How to Fix Any Real Estate Problem in 3 Minutes

by Brian P. Bagnall

BULLSHIT. That's what you might be thinking about whether this book can tell you how to fix any real estate problem in 3 minutes or less. Let me prove it to you.

It will take 30 seconds to read this page and the next that will tell you how everything works. Then find your problem from the list below and go to the page indicated and read a few pages that will tell you the action plan of how to fix the problem (there may be a flowchart in between). This will take you 2 or 3 minutes.

There it is, the solution in 3 minutes. That doesn't mean that you'll fix any real estate problem in 3 minutes, it means you'll know HOW to fix your problem within 3 minutes.

This book isn't meant to be read cover to cover. This is a reference manual to help you find a solution to your problem fast. You just read the parts that make sense for your situation.

A few tips:
1. Whatever situation you're in, the worst thing you can do is to sit there and not do anything. That's why I wrote this book. To provide you with a solution in clear and certain terms. Because that's the #1 reason folks don't do anything… because they don't have a clear path. Now you'll have it.
2. You have to be honest with yourself about where you're at. If you're in foreclosure, for instance, don't think that the bank/government can't take your property from you if you are behind on your mortgage or taxes or that a bag of money is going to magically show up on your doorstep that will help you solve all of your problems. You can hope for the best but you need to make decisions based in reality and have a plan. (just in case that magic bag of money doesn't show up).

If you at all doubt that I know real estate, go to www.BriansDeeds.com and look at dozens of deeds to properties I've bought over the years.

➤ **GO TO THE NEXT PAGE AND SELECT YOUR PROBLEM AND I WILL TELL YOU HOW TO SOLVE IT**

If you at all doubt that I know real estate, go to www.BriansDeeds.com and look at dozens of deeds to properties I've bought over the years.

Even though I've bought hundreds of properties over the last 20 years, I need to let you know that I'm not an attorney and I can't give you legal advice. That doesn't mean I don't know what I'm talking about though. :)

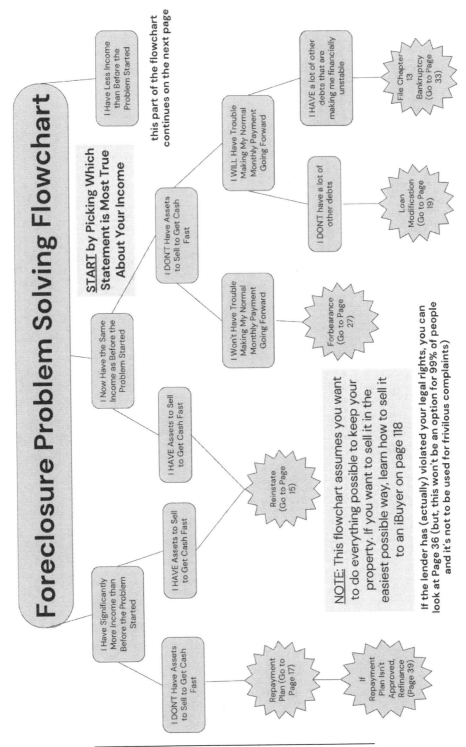

Foreclosure Problem Solving Flowchart

START by Picking Which Statement is Most True About Your Income

this part of the flowchart continues on the next page

- I Have Less Income than Before the Problem Started

- I Now Have the Same Income as Before the Problem Started
  - I DONT Have Assets to Sell to Get Cash Fast
    - I WILL Have Trouble Making My Normal Monthly Payment Going Forward
      - I HAVE a lot of other debts that are making me financially unstable → File Chapter 13 Bankruptcy (Go to Page 33)
      - I DONT have a lot of other debts → Loan Modification (Go to Page 19)
    - I Won't Have Trouble Making My Normal Monthly Payment Going Forward → Forbearance (Go to Page 27)
  - I HAVE Assets to Sell to Get Cash Fast → Reinstate (Go to Page 15)

- I Have Significantly More Income than Before the Problem Started
  - I HAVE Assets to Sell to Get Cash Fast → Reinstate (Go to Page 15)
  - I DONT Have Assets to Sell to Get Cash Fast → Repayment Plan (Go to Page 17) → If Repayment Plan Isn't Approved, Refinance (Page 39)

NOTE: This flowchart assumes you want to do everything possible to keep your property. If you want to sell it in the easiest possible way, learn how to sell it to an iBuyer on page 118

NOTE: If the lender has (actually) violated your legal rights, you can look at Page 36 (but, this won't be an option for 99% of people and it's not to be used for frivilous complaints)

Foreclosure Problem Solving Flowchart

(continued from the previous page)

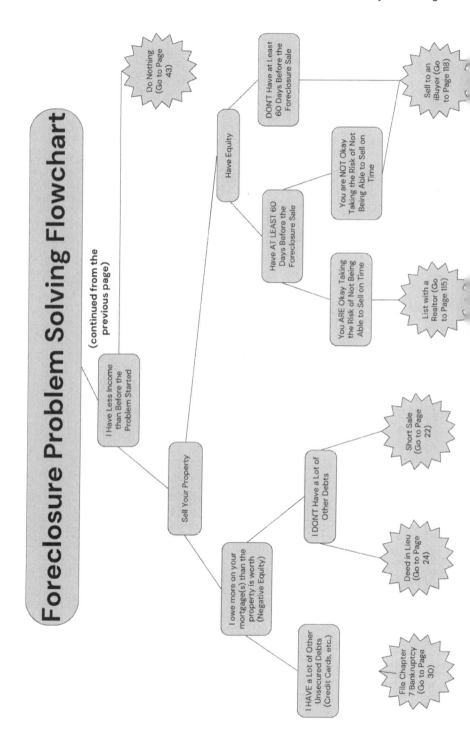

What Is Foreclosure?

Foreclosure is a legal process by which a lender, typically a bank or mortgage company, takes possession of a property from a homeowner who has failed to make mortgage payments as agreed upon in the mortgage contract.

The lender may then sell the property to recoup the outstanding mortgage debt and any other costs associated with the foreclosure process.

This process also applies to any other liens that are on your property (tax lien, mechanics lien, judgment lien, bail bond lien, municipal lien, etc.). Any lien holder that's not being paid can initiate foreclosure proceedings on your property.

Foreclosure can be a distressing and complex experience, with long-term consequences for your credit, finances, and overall well-being.

However, it's important to understand that you do have options and resources available to help you navigate this challenging situation.

In this section, we'll explore the options available to you, including steps they can take to potentially avoid foreclosure or mitigate its impact. The goal is to help you make informed decisions and take appropriate steps to protect your rights and financial interests.

It's important to approach the foreclosure process with knowledge, understanding, and proactive action to achieve the best possible outcome in this challenging situation.

We will cover the foreclosure process in detail, including the different stages involved, legal requirements, and timelines. We will also discuss various alternatives and strategies available to you.

It's important to note that foreclosure laws and regulations can vary significantly depending on the state and local laws, as well as the terms of the mortgage agreement.

To learn how to fix your foreclosure problem, please go to the Foreclosure Flowchart on page 5.

If you're thinking about selling your property, visit PAGE 118 so that you can hear how we might be able to make that a smooth process for you.

Foreclosure Timeline

Foreclosure is a legal process that varies depending on the state and local laws, as well as the terms of the mortgage agreement. However, the general foreclosure process typically involves several key steps.

Understanding these steps is crucial for you to navigate your options effectively:

Step 1: Missed Payments
Foreclosure typically begins when a homeowner fails to make mortgage payments as agreed upon in the mortgage contract. A lender can send a notice of default after as little as 1 missed payment, which is a formal notification stating that you are in breach of the mortgage contract. However, most lenders usually waits until at least 3 payments are missed.

Step 2: Pre-Foreclosure Period
After the notice of default, there is usually a pre-foreclosure period during which you have an opportunity to resolve the default and avoid foreclosure. During this period, you may be able to reinstate the loan by paying off the past-due amount, negotiate a loan modification, refinance the mortgage, or sell the property (among other options).

Step 3: Foreclosure Filing
If you are unable to resolve the default during the pre-foreclosure period, the lender may proceed with filing a foreclosure lawsuit or taking other legal action to initiate the foreclosure process. This typically involves filing a complaint or a notice of foreclosure with the court, which officially begins the foreclosure proceedings.

Step 4: Foreclosure Auction or Sale
Once the foreclosure process has been initiated, the property may be scheduled for a foreclosure auction or sale. This is typically conducted at a public auction, where the property is sold to the highest bidder. The proceeds from the sale are used to pay off the mortgage debt and any other liens or costs associated with the foreclosure process.

Step 5: Redemption Period (if applicable)

In some states, there may be a redemption period following the foreclosure sale, during which you have the right to reclaim the property by paying off the total mortgage debt, interest, and other costs. The length and availability of a redemption period vary depending on the state laws.

Step 6: Eviction (if applicable)

If you do not redeem the property during the redemption period, or if there is no redemption period, the new owner, usually the winning bidder at the foreclosure auction, may initiate eviction proceedings to remove you from the property.

To learn how to fix your foreclosure problem, please go to the Foreclosure Flowchart on page 5.

If you're thinking about selling your property, visit PAGE 118 so that you can hear how we might be able to make that a smooth process for you.

Foreclosure: Tips for Getting Through This

Foreclosure can be a complex and daunting process, but it's important for you to understand your rights and responsibilities throughout the process. In this chapter, we will discuss some key tips for protecting your rights and navigating the foreclosure process. It's important to approach it with a proactive mindset and explore all available options.

Don't Be Embarrassed
Financial challenges can happen to anyone. Financial difficulties can arise due to various reasons, such as job loss, medical emergencies, divorce, or other unforeseen circumstances. You aren't alone. Many people who face foreclosure may have had financial setbacks that were beyond their control. Being in foreclosure isn't a personal failure or a reflection of your character or worth. It's just a legal process that is governed by laws and regulations, and many homeowners find themselves in this situation.

Open Communication
Recognizing that you may need help during a foreclosure and taking proactive steps to seek assistance is admirable. It shows that you are taking responsibility for your situation and looking for solutions. The first step in negotiating with your lender during foreclosure is to establish open and honest communication. Contact your lender as soon as you realize that you may be facing foreclosure and express your willingness to work out a resolution. Be responsive to their communications and provide them with accurate and updated information about your financial situation.

Respond to Notices and Communications
It's crucial to respond promptly and thoroughly to any notices or communications you receive from your lender or other parties involved in the foreclosure process. Ignoring or delaying responses to notices can result in the loss of important rights and options. If you have questions or concerns about the notices or communications you receive, seek clarification from your lender.

If You Have Moved or Will Move Out of the Property

If you have moved out or plan to move out of the property, do not share this fact with your lender, as it may limit your options or accelerate the foreclosure.

Beware of Scams and Fraudulent Schemes

Unfortunately, there are scammers and fraudulent schemes that prey on vulnerable homeowners facing foreclosure. Beware of anyone who promises to stop or delay foreclosure in exchange for upfront fees or unrealistic guarantees.

DON'T DO NOTHING

Ignoring foreclosure is not a wise approach, as it can have serious consequences. If you ignore foreclosure notices or fail to respond to legal proceedings, you may lose important legal rights and protections that could have helped you in the foreclosure process. Ignoring foreclosure can result in significant financial losses as well. When a property is foreclosed upon, it is typically sold at a public auction or through a private sale, often at a price lower than the outstanding mortgage debt. This may result in a deficiency, which is the difference between the sale proceeds and the remaining mortgage balance. Ignoring foreclosure can lead to a higher deficiency amount, which may result in a judgment against you, wage garnishment, or other collection actions that last far beyond the actual foreclosure. Foreclosure has a significant impact on your credit score and credit history as well. A foreclosure remains on your credit report for several years and can severely impact your ability to qualify for future loans, credit cards, or favorable interest rates. Ignoring foreclosure can further damage your credit and make it challenging to rebuild your credit in the future. Foreclosure can also be a stressful and emotionally challenging experience. Ignoring foreclosure and avoiding dealing with the situation can lead to prolonged stress, anxiety, and uncertainty, which can take a toll on your mental and emotional well-being.

It's a Chance for a Fresh Start

While foreclosure can be a challenging experience, it can also be an opportunity for a fresh start. It's a chance to evaluate your financial situation, learn from any mistakes or missteps, and take steps towards rebuilding your financial future.

To learn how to fix your foreclosure problem, please go to the Foreclosure Flowchart on page 5.

If you're thinking about selling your property, visit PAGE 118 so that you can hear how we might be able to make that a smooth process for you.

I'm Having Trouble Keeping Up with My Payments and/or Property Expenses

Anyone can hit rough times and find it hard to financially keep up. I'm sorry that's happening to you.

If you ARE already behind on your payments, go to page 4 to read up on your options.

If you AREN'T already behind on your payments, continue reading this page.

Unless you can change something very quickly with your financial situation, the best bet is usually to sell your property so that you don't end up behind on your mortgage which really creates an avalanche of big problems. Once you're in foreclosure, it's hard to get out of.

Since you're probably going to want financial relief sooner rather than later, it usually eliminates the traditional options like selling for sale by owner (FSBO) or with an agent because those options can take months.

An iBuyer is probably your only possibility. You can sell your property fast and, if your property is in good condition and you're flexible on terms, an iBuyer can even put your money in your pocket than an agent can.

If you're open to selling through an iBuyer, visit page 118 so that you can hear how I might be able to make that a smooth process for you.

Reinstatement

Reinstatement involves bringing the mortgage current by paying off the total amount of past-due payments, late fees, attorney's fees and any other costs associated with the default all in one lump sum.

However, it's important to be aware that lenders may have specific deadlines and requirements for reinstatement, and failing to meet these requirements may result in the foreclosure process continuing.

This can be a viable option if you have the means to come up with the necessary funds in a lump sum. Reinstatement is something you would work it out with the lender directly.

Typically you won't have the cash on-hand in your checking or savings account to reinstate the loan but you might be able to take money out of your 401k or IRA (or possibly take a loan from one of those accounts). You can also sell things you have to bring in some cash.

Here are things that you can liquidate to provide cash:
- Cars (with or without loans)
- RVs/Motorhomes (with or without loans)
- Second Homes (with or without loans)
- Precious Metals (silver, gold, etc.)
- Jewelry
- Life insurance policy

If you have any of the first 4 things on the list that you want to liquidate for cash quickly, send me a text to (423) 460-6111 with the following information (text only for this service, please):
- Let me know you're trying to come up with funds to reinstate your loan so that I know what we're working with.
- Let me know what exactly you have and what kind of condition it's in.

And I may buy those things from you or know someone that will. Keep in mind that myself or my referrals will need a discount and can't buy at retail value.

If you're thinking about selling your property, visit PAGE 118 so that you can hear how I might be able to make that a smooth process for you.

If this solution didn't help or you think it won't work for you, return back to the Foreclosure Flowchart on page 5.

Repayment Plan/Reinstatement Plan

A lender repayment plan, also known as a reinstatement plan or a repayment agreement, is a negotiated agreement between you and your lender to resolve a delinquent mortgage and bring it current. It's one of the options you have to catch up on your overdue payments and prevent foreclosure.

The repayment plan may vary depending on the lender's policies and your financial situation, but it generally involves paying a portion of the overdue amount each month, along with the regular mortgage payments, until the delinquent balance is paid off.

This can be a financial strain, especially for homeowners who are already struggling with financial difficulties that led to the foreclosure in the first place so it's usually reserved for those homeowners that are actually making more income now than they were before the problem started (for example, maybe you found yourself in foreclosure because you lost your job for a few months but then you found another job that paid more than your last job).

Lender repayment plans can often be negotiated and customized based on your financial situation. This may allow for flexibility in terms of the repayment schedule, the amount of overdue payments to be paid, and the length of the repayment period. It provides an opportunity for you to work with your lender to come up with a plan that fits your budget.

Avoiding foreclosure through a repayment plan may help protect your credit score to some extent. While late payments and delinquency may have already impacted your credit score, preventing foreclosure and bringing the mortgage current can help limit further damage to your credit.

Not all homeowners qualify for a lender repayment plan. Lenders may have specific eligibility criteria, such as income requirements, credit history, and limitations on the amount of overdue payments, that must be met before a repayment plan can be agreed upon. If you do not meet these requirements, you may not be able to pursue a repayment plan as an option.

Depending on the amount of overdue payments and the terms of the repayment plan, catching up on delinquent payments within the agreed-upon timeframe may still be challenging for some homeowners. It's important to carefully assess your financial situation and budget to ensure that you can realistically meet the repayment plan requirements.

It's crucial to communicate with your lender as soon as possible if you are considering a lender repayment plan or any other option to resolve your foreclosure situation.

It's also important to make sure that you can agree to whatever plan you agree to or it can make matters worse. Don't agree to a pie-in-the-sky plan that would require all of the stars in the universe to align for you to hit the mark.

This solution is explored by contacting your lender directly.

Talking to your lender can be scary. I offer a service where I will talk to your lender, explain your situation and gather the options they are willing to do and present them to you. It's only $97 and well worth it. If this interests you, give me a call at (423) 460-6111 right now (day or night). If I don't answer, please leave a message so I know you called.

If you're thinking about selling your property, visit PAGE 118 so that you can hear how I might be able to make that a smooth process for you.

If this solution didn't help or you think it won't work for you, return back to the Foreclosure Flowchart on page 5.

Loan Modification

Loan modification is another option that homeowners can explore to avoid foreclosure. A loan modification is a renegotiation of the terms of the mortgage agreement, such as lowering the interest rate, extending the loan term or forgiving a portion of the principal balance, with the goal of making the monthly payments more affordable for the homeowner.

Loan modification typically requires submitting a formal application to the lender, providing financial documentation, and negotiating with the lender to reach a mutually agreeable modification. It's important to carefully review the terms of the loan modification and ensure that it is sustainable in the long term before proceeding,

Here are some potential positives of a loan modification:

1. *Lower Monthly Payments*: One of the main benefits of a loan modification is that it can result in lower monthly mortgage payments. A loan modification may involve lowering the interest rate, extending the loan term, or reducing the principal balance, which can result in a more affordable monthly payment.
2. *Avoidance of Foreclosure*: Loan modifications can help you avoid foreclosure, which is a legal process initiated by the lender to seize and sell the property due to default on the mortgage. By modifying the loan to make it more affordable, borrowers may be able to continue making payments and avoid the foreclosure process, thereby keeping their property.
3. *Potential Debt Forgiveness*: In some cases, a loan modification may involve forgiving a portion of the outstanding mortgage debt. This means that you may not be required to repay the full amount owed on the mortgage, which can provide significant financial relief and help you get back on track with your mortgage payments.

4. *Preservation of Credit Score*: A loan modification may have less impact on your credit score compared to a foreclosure or a short sale. While there may still be some negative impact on your credit score due to missed payments or changes in the loan terms, it may be less severe compared to the consequences of a foreclosure or a short sale.

Negatives of a Loan Modification:

1. *Lender Approval Required*: A loan modification requires approval from the lender, and there is no guarantee that the lender will agree to modify the loan. The lender may require extensive documentation, financial information, and may take time to review and approve the loan modification request.
2. *Possible Fees and Costs*: Some lenders charge fees for loan modifications, such as loan modification application fees, loan modification processing fees, or other costs associated with the modification process. These fees can add to the overall costs of the loan modification and may impact your financial situation.
3. *Potential Long-Term Costs*: While a loan modification may result in lower monthly payments, it can also result in additional long-term costs. For example, extending the loan term to lower the monthly payment may result in paying more interest over the life of the loan, which can increase the total cost of the mortgage.
4. *Impact on Credit Score*: While a loan modification may have less impact on the borrower's credit score compared to a foreclosure or a short sale, it can still have negative consequences. Late payments, missed payments, or changes in the loan terms may be reported to the credit bureaus and can result in a lower credit score.
5. *Potential for Emotional and Financial Stress*: Going through a loan modification process can be emotionally and financially stressful. It may involve extensive paperwork, communication with the lender, and uncertainty about the outcome. Additionally, the loan modification process may not result in a favorable outcome, and you may need to explore alternative options if a loan modification is not approved.

It's important for borrowers considering a loan modification to carefully evaluate their financial situation and fully understand the implications of a loan modification on their specific circumstances. It's essential to thoroughly review all terms and conditions of the loan modification agreement and ensure that it aligns with your financial goals and long-term financial sustainability.

Talking to your lender can be scary. I offer a service where I will talk to your lender, explain your situation and gather the options they are willing to do and present them to you. It's only $97 and well worth it. If this interests you, give me a call at (423) 460-6111 right now (day or night). If I don't answer, please leave a message so I know you called.

If you're thinking about selling your property, visit PAGE 118 so that you can hear how I might be able to make that a smooth process for you.

If this solution didn't help or you think it won't work for you, return back to the Foreclosure Flowchart on page 5.

Short Sale

A short sale is an option for homeowners who are behind on their payments and owe more on their mortgage than the current market value of their property. (basically, it means that your property is overleveraged)

In a short sale, the homeowner sells the property for less than the outstanding mortgage debt with the approval of the lender. The proceeds from the sale are then used to pay off the mortgage debt.

Short sales can often be completed more quickly than foreclosure proceedings, which can be a lengthy and complex process. By selling the property through a short sale, you may be able to resolve your financial situation more expeditiously and move on to a new chapter in your life.

Unlike a foreclosure, where the lender typically takes control of the sale process, with a short sale you have the opportunity to actively participate in the short sale process.

In a short sale, the lender must approve the sale and the offer price, as it may result in a loss for the lender. The lender may take time to review and approve the short sale, and there is no guarantee that they will agree to the terms or approve the sale at all.

Downsides:
1. *Possible Tax Implications:* The forgiveness of mortgage debt in a short sale may be considered taxable income by the IRS, and you may be required to report it as such. This can result in additional tax liabilities that you need to consider and plan for. (we can sometimes negotiate that the lender not report this as part of the deal but it's not guaranteed).

2. *Deficiency Judgment Possibility*: In some cases, the lender may reserve the right to pursue a deficiency judgment against you even after the short sale. This means that you may still be responsible for paying the remaining balance of the mortgage debt, which can result in financial obligations even after the sale of the property. (we can sometimes negotiate that the lender waive this as part of the deal but it's not guaranteed).

3. *Complicated*: There is a short sale package that must be presented to the lender and it can be complex. They request a lot of documentation: financials, hardship letter, repair estimates, comparable sales, net sheet, etc.) And you don't complete this packet until you have a buyer and a purchase agreement.

I buy short sale properties all of the time, so if you choose to go this route, you have a built-in buyer with me. That will make the process easier and I'll help you with all of the (complicated) paperwork too. You'll have more control of your sale date too which allows you to better prepare for the future.

To get help with a short sale or to sell your property, pickup the phone and give me (Brian) a call directly at (423) 460-6111. If I don't answer, please make sure you leave a voicemail message so that I know you called. (sometimes my phone doesn't have service and I won't see that you called).

If this solution didn't help or you think it won't work for you, return back to the Foreclosure Flowchart on page 5.

Deed in Lieu of Foreclosure

A deed in lieu of foreclosure is a voluntary agreement between the homeowner and the lender where the homeowner transfers the property to the lender in exchange for the release of the mortgage debt.

This option allows homeowners to avoid foreclosure and the associated legal costs, but it may have an impact on your credit score and could result in a deficiency judgment if the property's value does not cover the full mortgage debt.

There are positives and negatives to doing a deed in lieu of foreclosure.

Here are Some of the Positives:

1. *Potential Release from Liability*: In some cases, a lender may agree to release you from any further liability for the mortgage debt after a deed in lieu of foreclosure is completed, which means you may not be responsible for any deficiency amount.
2. *Expedited Process*: Compared to foreclosure, which involves legal proceedings, a deed in lieu of foreclosure can be a faster process, as it is a voluntary agreement between you and the lender.
3. *May Preserve Credit*: While a deed in lieu of foreclosure will have a negative impact on your credit, it may be less damaging than a foreclosure, as it is considered a voluntary action by you and not a forced sale by the lender.
4. *Potential Relocation Assistance*: Some lenders may offer relocation assistance or financial incentives to you if you complete a deed in lieu of foreclosure, which can help ease the transition to alternative housing arrangements.

Negatives of a Deed in Lieu of Foreclosure:

1. *Credit Impact*: While a deed in lieu of foreclosure may be less damaging to your credit than a foreclosure, it will still have a negative impact on your credit, potentially lowering your credit score and making it harder to obtain credit in the future.
2. *Surrender of Property*: By completing a deed in lieu of foreclosure, you voluntarily transfer the title of the property to the lender, which means losing ownership and possession of the property.
3. *Potential Deficiency Liability*: In some cases, the lender may reserve the right to pursue a deficiency judgment against you for any remaining balance on the mortgage debt after the property is transferred through a deed in lieu of foreclosure. This can result in further financial obligations for the homeowner.
4. *Impact on Future Homeownership*: A deed in lieu of foreclosure may have implications for your ability to obtain financing or qualify for a new mortgage in the future, as it will typically be reported on your credit history and may affect your eligibility for certain loan programs.
5. *Voluntary Agreement*: Unlike foreclosure, which is a legal process initiated by the lender, a deed in lieu of foreclosure is a voluntary agreement between you and the lender. This means that you must actively negotiate and obtain the lender's approval for a deed in lieu of foreclosure, and not all lenders may be willing to accept this option.

It's important to carefully consider the specific circumstances of your situation before deciding whether a deed in lieu of foreclosure is the right option for you. Each case is unique, and the potential positives and negatives of a deed in lieu of foreclosure can vary depending on factors such as your financial situation, the lender's policies, and the state's laws and regulations.

Talking to your lender can be scary. I offer a service where I will talk to your lender, explain your situation and gather the options they are willing to do and present them to you. It's only $97 and well worth it. If this interests you, give me a call at (423) 460-6111 right now (day or night). If I don't answer, please leave a message so I know you called.

If you're thinking about getting rid of your property, selling it outright to an iBuyer might be a better solution in some circumstances but you must be open to creative solutions. Visit PAGE 118 so that you can hear how I might be able to make that a smooth process for you.

If this solution didn't help or you think it won't work for you, return back to the Foreclosure Flowchart on page 5.

Forbearance

Forbearance is an agreement between you and the lender that allows you to temporarily suspend or reduce your mortgage payments for a specific period of time. Forbearance is typically granted in cases of temporary financial hardship, such as a job loss or a medical emergency. It's also typically offered by lenders during a natural disaster.

However, it's important to note that forbearance is not a permanent solution and you will be required to make up the missed payments or negotiate a repayment plan with the lender after the forbearance period ends.

Here are some potential positives of forbearance:

1. *Short-term Relief:* Forbearance can provide short-term relief for borrowers who are facing financial difficulties and are unable to make their full mortgage payments. It can allow borrowers to temporarily pause or reduce their mortgage payments, which can provide breathing room during a period of financial hardship.
2. *Avoidance of Default:* By granting forbearance, lenders may help borrowers avoid defaulting on their mortgage, which is a situation where the borrower fails to make timely payments as per the loan agreement. Defaulting on a mortgage can have severe consequences, including foreclosure, which can result in the loss of the property.
3. *Flexibility and Customization:* Forbearance plans can be customized to meet the specific needs of the borrower, depending on their financial situation and the nature of the hardship. Lenders may offer different types of forbearance plans, such as partial forbearance (reduced payments), full forbearance (no payments), or graduated forbearance (gradually increasing payments), to accommodate the borrower's circumstances.

4. *Credit Reporting*: During forbearance, some lenders may report the borrower's account as current to the credit bureaus, which means that the borrower's credit score may not be negatively impacted. This can help borrowers protect their credit score and maintain a good credit history, which can be important for their financial future.

Negatives of Forbearance:

1. *Accrued Interest and Fees*: During forbearance, the borrower's mortgage payments may be reduced or paused, but the interest on the outstanding balance continues to accrue. This means that the borrower may owe more in total mortgage payments over the life of the loan, as well as additional fees associated with the forbearance, depending on the lender's policies.
2. *Temporary Relief, Not Permanent Solution*: Forbearance is typically a temporary relief option and not a permanent solution to the borrower's financial difficulties. At the end of the forbearance period, the borrower may be required to repay the deferred or reduced payments, along with any accrued interest and fees, which can result in higher monthly payments or a lump sum payment.
3. *Eligibility and Approval*: Forbearance is not automatically granted to all borrowers and requires approval from the lender. Lenders may have specific eligibility criteria and documentation requirements that borrowers must meet to qualify for forbearance. Not all borrowers may be eligible for forbearance, and the lender's decision may depend on the borrower's financial situation and the nature of the hardship.
4. *Impact on Credit Score*: While some lenders may not report forbearance to the credit bureaus as negative, it may still impact the borrower's credit score in certain cases. For example, if the lender reports the borrower's account as in forbearance, it may be reflected on the credit report and could potentially impact the borrower's credit score, although not as severely as a default or foreclosure.

5. *Long-term Financial Implications*: Forbearance may provide temporary relief, but it does not eliminate the borrower's obligation to repay the deferred or reduced payments, along with any accrued interest and fees. This means that the borrower may face higher monthly payments or a lump sum payment at the end of the forbearance period, which could impact their long-term financial stability.

It's important for borrowers considering forbearance to fully understand the terms and conditions of the forbearance agreement, including the repayment terms, interest accrual, and fees.

Talking to your lender can be scary. I offer a service where I will talk to your lender, explain your situation and gather the options they are willing to do and present them to you. It's only $97 and well worth it. If this interests you, give me a call at (423) 460-6111 right now (day or night). If I don't answer, please leave a message so I know you called.

If you're thinking about selling your property, visit PAGE 118 so that you can hear how I might be able to make that a smooth process for you.

If this solution didn't help or you think it won't work for you, return back to the Foreclosure Flowchart on page 5.

Foreclosure: File for Chapter 7 Bankruptcy

In some cases, foreclosure may be accompanied by financial challenges that may require you to consider bankruptcy as an option. Bankruptcy can have a significant impact on your financial situation, and it's important to seek professional legal advice before making any decisions.

Filing for bankruptcy during foreclosure can have both positive and negative consequences, depending on your specific circumstances.

Positives of Filing for Bankruptcy during Foreclosure:

1. *Automatic Stay*: One of the main benefits of filing for bankruptcy is that it triggers an automatic stay, which is a legal order that halts all collection actions, including foreclosure proceedings. This can provide immediate relief to you by stopping the foreclosure process and giving you time to assess your financial situation and explore potential options to save your property.
2. *Discharge of Debts*: Chapter 7 bankruptcy allows for the discharge of certain unsecured debts, such as credit card debt, medical bills, and personal loans. This can free up your financial resources and help you focus on resolving your foreclosure issue.
3. *Protection of Other Assets*: Bankruptcy can also provide protection for other assets, such as personal property or savings accounts, from being seized by creditors. This can help you retain some financial stability and potentially safeguard your other assets from being liquidated.
4. *Fresh Start*: Chapter 7 bankruptcy is often referred to as a "fresh start" bankruptcy because it allows you to eliminate or reduce your debt burden, giving you a chance to rebuild your financial future without the weight of unmanageable debts.

Negatives of Filing for Bankruptcy during Foreclosure:

1. *Impact on Credit*: Filing for Chapter 7 bankruptcy will have a negative impact on your credit score and will remain on your credit report for up to 10 years. This can make it more challenging to obtain credit in the future and may affect your ability to secure loans, rent a home, or even find employment.

2. *Foreclosure Still Possible*: While the automatic stay can temporarily halt foreclosure proceedings, it's important to note that Chapter 7 bankruptcy does not guarantee that you will be able to keep your property. If you are significantly behind on your mortgage and unable to catch up soon, the lender may seek relief from the automatic stay and proceed with the foreclosure.

3. *Legal and Filing Fees*: Filing for bankruptcy involves various legal and filing fees, which can add to the financial burden of you being behind on your mortgage. These fees can vary depending on the type of bankruptcy filed and the complexity of the case, and may need to be paid upfront.

4. *Loss of Non-exempt Assets*: Chapter 7 bankruptcy involves liquidating non-exempt assets to repay creditors. If you have valuable assets that are not protected by bankruptcy exemptions, they may be sold to repay your debts, including your mortgage. This could potentially result in the loss of property, including your home, if it is not protected by exemptions.

5. *Potential for Mortgage Reaffirmation*: In a Chapter 7 bankruptcy, you may be required to reaffirm the mortgage debt, which means they will still be responsible for repaying the full amount of the mortgage debt even after the bankruptcy discharge. This may not be feasible for some homeowners, especially if they are already struggling with financial difficulties.

6. *Public Record*: Bankruptcy filings are public records, which means that your financial situation and bankruptcy status may become a matter of public record. This lack of privacy can be a disadvantage for you if you who wish to keep their financial situation confidential.

An attorney can help you understand the different types of bankruptcy, assess your eligibility, and navigate the complex legal process. It's important to note that bankruptcy laws and procedures can be complex and vary by jurisdiction.

Therefore, it's crucial to consult with a qualified bankruptcy attorney who can assess your individual financial situation, explain the potential consequences of filing for Chapter 7 bankruptcy during foreclosure, and help you navigate the bankruptcy process effectively.

Additionally, it's important to consider all available options, including alternatives to bankruptcy, and weigh the pros and cons before making a decision.

Attorneys can be sharks (and not always in a good way). If you'd like a referral to a trusted and proven Bankruptcy Attorney in my network, send me a text to (423) 460-6111 and let me know (please, text only for this service).

If you choose Chapter 7 Bankruptcy, you may have to sell your property. If you do, visit page 118 so that you can hear how I might be able to make that a smooth process for you and get the Bankruptcy over with quicker.

If this solution didn't help or you think it won't work for you, return back to the Foreclosure Flowchart on page 5.

Foreclosure: Filing for Chapter 13 Bankruptcy

Filing for Chapter 13 bankruptcy during foreclosure can have both positives and negatives, and it's crucial to carefully evaluate your financial situation and consult with a qualified bankruptcy attorney before making any decisions.

Positives of filing Chapter 13 bankruptcy during foreclosure:

1. *Automatic Stay*: Filing for Chapter 13 bankruptcy triggers an automatic stay, which temporarily halts foreclosure proceedings. This provides you with immediate relief from the stress of foreclosure and an opportunity to develop a repayment plan to catch up on your mortgage payments over time.
2. *Repayment Plan*: Chapter 13 bankruptcy allows you to propose a repayment plan to catch up on your mortgage arrears over a period of three to five years. This can provide you with a structured and manageable plan to repay your past-due mortgage payments while keeping your property.
3. *Protecting Your Assets*: Chapter 13 bankruptcy allows you to retain ownership and possession of your assets, including your property, while you work on repaying your debts through the court-approved repayment plan. This can provide you with the opportunity to save your property from foreclosure and keep your other assets as well.
4. *Debt Consolidation*: Chapter 13 bankruptcy consolidates your debts into a single repayment plan, which can make it more manageable to repay your creditors, including your mortgage lender. This can help you regain control of your finances and create a plan to catch up on your mortgage payments and other debts over time.
5. *Improved Credit Standing*: While Chapter 13 bankruptcy will have a negative impact on your credit score, it is considered less damaging than Chapter 7 bankruptcy and typically remains on your credit report for seven years. As you make regular payments under the court-approved repayment plan, it may help improve your credit standing over time.

Negatives of filing Chapter 13 bankruptcy during foreclosure:

1. *Repayment Plan Requirements*: Filing for Chapter 13 bankruptcy requires you to propose a court-approved repayment plan and make regular payments over a period of three to five years. This may require significant financial discipline and may limit your discretionary spending during the repayment period. If you are unable to make the required monthly payments, your bankruptcy case may be dismissed, and the foreclosure process may resume.
2. *Lengthy Process*: Chapter 13 bankruptcy is a long-term commitment, typically lasting three to five years, during which you are required to make regular payments under the court-approved repayment plan. This can be a significant time commitment and may require you to adhere to a strict budget and financial plan for an extended period.
3. *Impact on Credit*: Filing Chapter 13 bankruptcy will have a negative impact on your credit score, and it will remain on your credit report for several years. This may affect your ability to obtain credit in the future, including loans, credit cards, and other forms of credit.
4. *Public Record*: Chapter 13 bankruptcy is a public record, and your filing will be recorded in public records accessible to the public, which may impact your privacy and financial reputation.

It's important to note that bankruptcy laws and procedures can be complex and vary by jurisdiction. Therefore, it's crucial to consult with a qualified bankruptcy attorney who can assess your individual financial situation, explain the potential consequences of filing for Chapter 13 bankruptcy during foreclosure, and help you navigate the bankruptcy process effectively.

Additionally, it's important to consider all available options, including alternatives to bankruptcy, and weigh the pros and cons before making a decision.

Attorneys can be sharks (and not always in a good way). If you'd like a referral to a trusted and proven Bankruptcy Attorney in my network, send me a text to (423) 460-6111 and let me know. (please, text only for this service)

If you choose Chapter 13 Bankruptcy, you may have to sell your property. If you do, visit page 118 so that you can hear how I might be able to make that a smooth process for you and get the Bankruptcy over with quicker.

If this solution didn't help or you think it won't work for you, return back to the Foreclosure Flowchart on page 5.

Foreclosure Legal Defenses

Homeowners facing foreclosure may also have legal defenses available to them, depending on the specific circumstances of their case. This may include challenging the validity of the foreclosure proceedings, asserting violations of mortgage laws or regulations, or seeking legal representation to negotiate with the lender.

Fighting a foreclosure in court can be a complex and challenging process, but it may be an option for you if you believe the foreclosure is unjust or unlawful.

You should take note that many homeowners froth at the idea of going after their lender in court but 99% don't have an actual case and end up disappointed. There's also attorney costs to consider which can quickly exceed the amount that is past due on your mortgage.

Here are some general steps to consider when fighting a foreclosure in court:

1. *Understand the Foreclosure Laws in Your State*: Foreclosure laws vary by state, so it's important to understand the specific laws and regulations in your state. Familiarize yourself with the foreclosure process, including the timelines, notice requirements, and legal procedures that must be followed in your state.
2. *Review Your Mortgage Documents*: Carefully review your mortgage documents, including the loan agreement, promissory note, and any other relevant paperwork. Look for any violations of federal or state lending laws, such as predatory lending practices, improper disclosure of terms, or other violations that may be relevant to your case.
3. *Seek Legal Representation*: Fighting a foreclosure in court can be complicated, and it's highly recommended to seek legal representation from an experienced foreclosure defense attorney. A skilled attorney can provide you with legal advice, represent you in court, and help you navigate the complexities of the legal system.

4. *Respond to Foreclosure Notices and Court Summons*: If you receive a foreclosure notice or court summons, it's crucial to respond within the required timeframe. Failure to respond may result in a default judgment in favor of the lender. Your attorney can help you draft and file the appropriate legal documents in response to the foreclosure notice or court summons.

5. *Raise Valid Defenses*: In court, you may be able to raise valid defenses to challenge the foreclosure. Common defenses include fraud, breach of contract, lack of standing, improper notice, violations of federal or state lending laws, and other legal issues. Your attorney can help you identify and raise the appropriate defenses based on the facts and circumstances of your case.

6. *Attend Court Hearings and Mediation Sessions*: Be prepared to attend court hearings and mediation sessions as required. Your attorney will represent you in court and present your defenses, and you may be required to provide evidence and testify on your behalf. Be prompt, professional, and prepared to present your case effectively.

7. *Explore Settlement Options*: In some cases, lenders may be open to settlement options, such as loan modifications, forbearance agreements, or other alternatives to foreclosure. Your attorney can help negotiate with the lender to explore possible settlement options that may allow you to keep your property or avoid foreclosure.

8. *Be Diligent and Persistent*: Fighting a foreclosure in court can be a lengthy and challenging process, requiring diligence and persistence. Stay in regular communication with your attorney, follow all court deadlines, and provide any requested information or documentation promptly. Be prepared for the legal process to take time and be prepared for potential setbacks along the way.

9. *Keep Records and Documentation*: Keep detailed records of all communication, documents, and evidence related to your foreclosure case. This includes correspondence with the lender, court documents, legal filings, and any other relevant information. Having organized and comprehensive records can be crucial in building your case and presenting your defenses in court.

It's important to note that foreclosure laws and legal procedures can be complex and may require expert legal guidance. It's highly recommended to seek assistance from an experienced foreclosure defense attorney who can provide you with personalized advice and representation based on the specific circumstances of your case. Remember to act promptly and diligently, and be prepared for a potentially lengthy legal process.

Attorneys can be sharks (and not always in a good way). If you'd like a referral to a trusted and proven Bankruptcy Attorney in my network, send me a text to (423) 460-6111 and let me know. (please, text only for this service)

If you're thinking about selling your property, visit page 118 so that you can hear how I might be able to make that a smooth process for you.

If this solution didn't help or you think it won't work for you, return back to the Foreclosure Flowchart on page 5.

Refinancing in Foreclosure

Refinancing during foreclosure is generally challenging as it may be difficult for borrowers in foreclosure to qualify for a new loan due to their financial situation and credit history.

Sometimes the only people that will refinance you after you are behind on your mortgage are private lenders. Private lenders will charge you very high interest rates and you must have a significant amount of equity in your property.

Here are some potential positives and negatives of refinancing during foreclosure:

Positives of Refinancing During Foreclosure:

1. *Consolidation of Debt*: Refinancing may allow you to consolidate other debts, such as credit card debts or personal loans, into the new mortgage. This could potentially help you manage your debts more effectively and improve your overall financial situation.
2. *Extension of Loan Term*: Refinancing may allow you to extend the term of your loan, which could result in lower monthly payments. This could provide some relief to your financial situation during the foreclosure process.
3. *Potential to Save the Property*: If you are able to refinance and use the proceeds to pay off the delinquent mortgage, it may help you catch up on your payments and potentially save your property from foreclosure. Refinancing could provide a way for you to repay the outstanding debt and reinstate your mortgage.

Negatives of Refinancing During Foreclosure:

1. *Difficulty in Qualifying*: Borrowers in foreclosure may have a tarnished credit history and may be considered high-risk borrowers by lenders. This could make it difficult for you to qualify for a new loan, especially with favorable terms and conditions. Lenders may require a higher credit score, a larger down payment, or additional documentation and proof of financial stability, which could be challenging for those in foreclosure.
2. *Higher Interest Rates or Fees*: Lenders may charge higher interest rates or fees for borrowers in foreclosure due to the increased risk involved. This could result in higher monthly payments or overall costs of the loan, which may not provide significant relief to the borrower's financial situation.
3. *Limited Options*: Refinancing options may be limited for borrowers in foreclosure, as many lenders may be unwilling to extend new loans to borrowers in financial distress. This could reduce your chances of finding a suitable refinancing option that meets your needs.
4. *Additional Costs*: Refinancing during foreclosure may also come with additional costs, such as appraisal fees, closing costs, or prepayment penalties, which could add to your overall financial burden.
5. *Potential Loss of Home*: If you are unable to qualify for refinancing during foreclosure or are unable to repay the delinquent mortgage with the proceeds of the new loan, you may still face the risk of losing your property to foreclosure. Refinancing is not a guaranteed solution to save the property, and borrowers should carefully assess their financial situation and the terms of the new loan before proceeding.

It's important for borrowers in foreclosure to carefully consider the potential positives and negatives of refinancing and seek professional advice from a qualified mortgage professional to determine if it's a viable option for their specific situation.

Finding a private lender to refinance your mortgage can be challenging, as private lenders are not as widely advertised or readily available as traditional lenders such as banks or credit unions.

However, here are some tips on how you might be able to find a private lender for mortgage refinancing:

1. *Network and Word of Mouth*: Start by asking your family, friends, colleagues, or acquaintances if they know of any private lenders or have any recommendations. Networking and word of mouth can be a valuable way to find potential private lenders who may not be advertising their services openly.

2. *Real Estate Investment Clubs or Associations*: Joining real estate investment clubs or associations in your local area can be a good way to connect with private lenders who may be interested in mortgage financing. These clubs or associations often bring together real estate investors, including private lenders, who are looking for investment opportunities.

3. *Online Platforms*: There are online platforms that connect borrowers with private lenders, and some of them may specialize in mortgage refinancing. Research and explore reputable online platforms that facilitate private lending transactions and connect borrowers with potential lenders.

4. *Attorney or Financial Advisor Referrals*: Attorneys or financial advisors who specialize in real estate or mortgage matters may have connections to private lenders or be able to refer you to reputable private lenders who may be able to assist with mortgage refinancing.

5. *Local Real Estate Professionals*: Local real estate professionals such as real estate agents, mortgage brokers, or property managers may have connections to private lenders who may be interested in financing mortgage refinancing deals. Reach out to these professionals and inquire if they have any recommendations or contacts.

6. *Online Searches*: Conduct online searches using relevant keywords such as "private mortgage lenders," "private mortgage refinance," or "private lenders for mortgage refinancing." Be sure to research and carefully vet any potential lenders you find online to ensure their credibility and legitimacy.

7. *Local Business Directories*: Check local business directories or the Yellow Pages for private lenders who may operate in your area.

It's important to exercise caution and thoroughly research any potential private lenders before proceeding with a mortgage refinance. Private lenders may have different lending criteria, terms, and interest rates compared to traditional lenders, so be sure to carefully review and understand the terms of the loan before committing to any agreement.

It's also advisable to seek legal and financial advice from qualified professionals to ensure that you make informed decisions throughout the process of finding and working with a private lender for mortgage refinancing.

If you need a referral to someone that might be able to get you refinanced, please send me a text to (423) 460-6111 and let me know your needs. (please, text only for this service).

If you're thinking about selling your property, visit page 118 so that you can hear how I might be able to make that a smooth process for you.

If this solution didn't help or you think it won't work for you, return back to the Foreclosure Flowchart on page 5.

Foreclosure: Doing Nothing

There's very little advice that I can give with 100% certainty without knowing your specific situation. But this is one of those pieces of advice that applies to everyone: *DOING NOTHING IS THE WORST THING YOU CAN DO.*

If you do nothing, you get the full force of the foreclosure process and there's no way to soften any blows.

If the bank forecloses on your property, it means that the lender has taken legal action to enforce their right to seize and sell your property due to your default on the mortgage loan.

The specific process and consequences of a foreclosure can vary depending on the laws and regulations of your state or jurisdiction, as well as the terms and conditions of your mortgage agreement.

However, in general, the following may happen if the bank forecloses on your property and you don't do anything:

1. *Foreclosure Deficiency Judgment*: A foreclosure deficiency judgment is a legal judgment issued by a court that holds a borrower personally liable for the remaining balance on a mortgage loan after a foreclosure sale has taken place and the proceeds from the sale are insufficient to cover the outstanding loan balance, including any accrued interest, fees, and costs. In other words, if you go through foreclosure and the sale of the foreclosed property does not generate enough proceeds to fully satisfy the outstanding mortgage debt, the lender may seek a deficiency judgment to recover the remaining amount from the you personally. The lender can pursue collection actions, such as wage garnishment, bank account levies, or property liens, to recover the deficiency amount from your personal assets.

2. *Damaged Credit*: With a full blown foreclosure on your record, you will have maximum damage to your credit. A foreclosure is a derogatory mark on your credit report and can stay on your credit history for up to seven years or more. This can make it challenging to obtain credit in the future, such as loans, credit cards, or mortgages, and may result in higher interest rates or less favorable terms if you are approved for credit.

3. *Possible Tax Implications:* The forgiveness of mortgage debt may be considered taxable income by the IRS, and you may be required to report it as such. This can result in additional tax liabilities that you need to consider and plan for.

4. *Impact on Future Homeownership*: A foreclosure may have implications on your ability to obtain financing or qualify for a new mortgage in the future, as it will typically be reported on your credit history and may affect your eligibility for certain loan programs.

5. *Loss of Ownership*: The most significant consequence of a foreclosure is the loss of ownership of your property. Once the foreclosure process is completed, the bank or lender becomes the legal owner of the property, and you are required to vacate the premises.

6. *Eviction*: If you do not voluntarily vacate the property after the foreclosure, the bank may initiate eviction proceedings to legally remove you from the property. Eviction is a legal process that typically involves court proceedings and can result in the involvement of law enforcement to forcibly remove you from the property.

7. *Loss of Equity*: If you have built up equity in your property, which is the difference between the market value of the property and the remaining mortgage balance, a foreclosure may result in the loss of that equity. The bank typically sells the foreclosed property at a foreclosure auction or through other means, and the proceeds are used to satisfy the outstanding mortgage debt, legal fees, and other costs associated with the foreclosure process. If the proceeds are not enough to cover the debt, you may lose your equity in the property.

8. *Emotional and Psychological Impact*: Going through a foreclosure can also have emotional and psychological impacts. Losing your property, facing eviction, and dealing with the financial and legal consequences of foreclosure can be stressful, emotionally draining, and may impact your overall well-being and quality of life.

If you now understand why doing nothing isn't really an option (and I hope you do), return back to the Foreclosure Flowchart on page 5. to see what your course of action should be.

If you're thinking about selling your property, visit page 118 so that you can hear how I might be able to make that a smooth process for you.

Delinquent Property Tax Flowchart

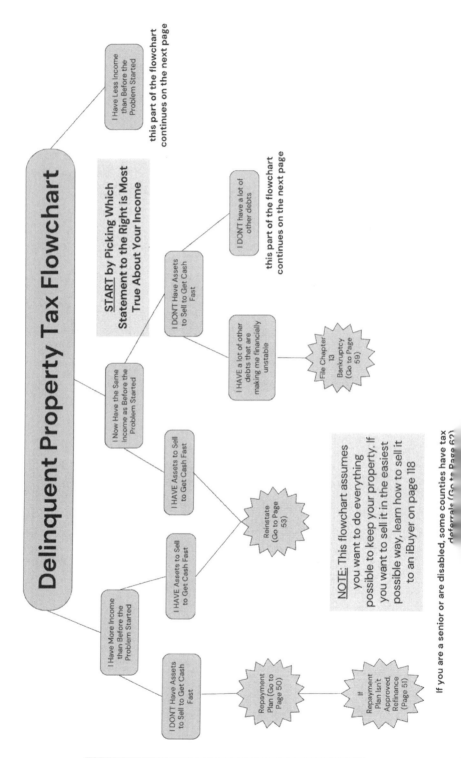

START by Picking Which Statement to the Right is Most True About Your Income

I Have Less Income than Before the Problem Started

this part of the flowchart continues on the next page

I Now Have the Same Income as Before the Problem Started

I DON'T Have Assets to Sell to Get Cash Fast

I DON'T have a lot of other debts

this part of the flowchart continues on the next page

I HAVE a lot of other debts that are making me financially unstable

File Chapter 13 Bankruptcy (Go to Page 59)

I HAVE Assets to Sell to Get Cash Fast

Reinstate (Go to Page 53)

I Have More Income than Before the Problem Started

I HAVE Assets to Sell to Get Cash Fast

I DON'T Have Assets to Sell to Get Cash Fast

Repayment Plan (Go to Page 50)

If Repayment Plan Isn't Approved, Refinance (Page 51)

NOTE: This flowchart assumes you want to do everything possible to keep your property. If you want to sell it in the easiest possible way, learn how to sell it to an iBuyer on page 118

If you are a senior or are disabled, some counties have tax deferral (Go to Page 62)

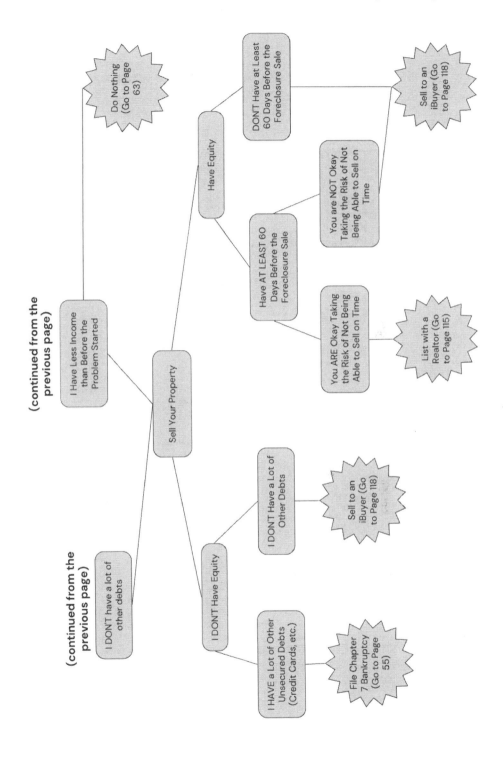

Unpaid Property Taxes Timeline

Here is a general timeline of what happens when your property taxes aren't paid:

Due date: Property taxes are typically due on a specific date each year, usually determined by the local government. Failure to pay the taxes by the due date will result in penalties and interest charges.

Delinquent status: After the due date has passed, the property taxes become delinquent. At this point, the local government may start sending notices or reminders about the unpaid taxes.

Late fees and interest: Most local governments will charge you late fees and interest on unpaid property taxes. These fees and interest can add up quickly, making it more difficult to pay off your debt.

Tax liens: After a certain period of time, typically a few months to a year, the local government can place a tax lien on your property. This means that they have a legal claim on your property until the taxes are paid. Tax liens can make it difficult to sell or refinance your property. Local governments have the authority to take legal action against you for failing to pay your property taxes. This can result in court judgments, wage garnishments, or bank account seizures.

Tax sale notification: If the taxes remain unpaid for an extended period of time, the local government may initiate the process of selling the property (or the right to seize the property) to collect the unpaid taxes. Typically, the property owner will receive a notification of the pending tax sale.

Tax sale auction: If the property taxes remain unpaid after the notification period has passed, the property may be sold at a public auction to satisfy the debt. The proceeds of the auction will be used to pay off the unpaid taxes, penalties, and interest, with any excess going to the property owner. This can result in the loss of your property, and you may not receive any proceeds from the sale.

Redemption period: In some cases, the property owner may be given a redemption period after the tax sale to pay off the delinquent taxes and reclaim the property. The length of the redemption period varies by state and local government. You should know that some counties don't offer redemption periods.

Eviction or forfeiture: If the property owner fails to redeem the property within the redemption period, the purchaser of the property at the tax sale may be entitled to evict the previous owner or initiate forfeiture proceedings to take possession of the property.

It's important to note that the specific timeline and procedures for unpaid property taxes can vary by state and local government. It's important to check with your local government to understand the specific process in your area.

In summary, failing to pay your property taxes can result in serious financial consequences, including late fees, tax liens, foreclosure (tax sale), and legal action. It's essential to take action to address any unpaid property taxes as soon as possible to avoid these negative outcomes.

If you're thinking about selling your property, visit page 118 so that you can hear how I might be able to make that a smooth process for you.

If you'd like to find the best solution for your delinquent property tax problem, please see page 46 for the delinquent tax flowchart.

Unpaid Property Taxes: Payment Plan

Many local governments offer payment plans for property taxes. These plans typically allow you to make monthly payments over an extended period.

This option should be exercised as soon as possible because, oftentimes, this option isn't available the further you get behind on property taxes.

Contact your local tax collector's office to see if they offer a payment plan and if you qualify for one.

Talking to the government can be scary. I offer a service where I will talk to your county, explain your situation and gather the options they are willing to do and present them to you. It's only $97 and well worth it. If this interests you, give me a call at (423) 460-6111 right now (day or night). If I don't answer, please leave a message so I know you called.

If you're thinking about selling your property, visit page 118 so that you can hear how I might be able to make that a smooth process for you.

If this solution didn't help or you think it won't work for you, return back to the Delinquent Property Tax Flowchart on page 46.

Unpaid Property Taxes: Refinance

You may be able to refinance your mortgage to include your property taxes. This can make it easier to manage your finances and ensure that your property taxes are paid on time.

Positives of Refinancing:

1. *Consolidation of Debt*: Refinancing may allow you to consolidate other debts, such as credit card debts or personal loans, into the new mortgage. This could potentially help you manage your debts more effectively and improve your overall financial situation.
2. *Extension of Loan Term*: Refinancing may allow you to extend the term of your loan, which could result in lower monthly payments. This could provide some relief to your financial situation.
3. *Potential to Save the Property*: If you are able to refinance and use the proceeds to pay off the delinquent taxes, it will help you save your property.

Negatives of Refinancing:

1. *Additional Costs*: Refinancing will come with additional costs, such as appraisal fees, closing costs, or prepayment penalties, which could add to your overall financial burden.
2. *Potential Loss of Property*: If you are unable to qualify for refinancing, you may still face the risk of losing your property. Refinancing is not a guaranteed solution to save the property, and you should carefully assess your financial situation and the terms of the new loan before proceeding.

It's important for folks behind on their property taxes to consider the potential positives and negatives of refinancing and seek professional advice from a qualified mortgage professional to determine if it's a viable option for their specific situation.

If you need a referral to someone that might be able to get you refinanced, please send me a text to (423) 460-6111 and let me know your needs. (please, text only for this service).

If you're thinking about selling your property, visit page 118 so that you can hear how I might be able to make that a smooth process for you.

If this solution didn't help or you think it won't work for you, return back to the Delinquent Property Tax Flowchart on page 46.

Unpaid Property Taxes: Find Money and Repay

Finding the money to pay off your past due property taxes is going to be one of the easiest options if you have the money or you can come up with it.

One of the best options is to look towards your 401k or IRA and see if you can take a distribution or loan from it. You may have to pay some penalties or interest (depending on which option you choose) but it's probably better than losing your property.

Selling things is another option if you have things available to sell. Contact your local tax collector's office to find out how much you owe so you know how much you need to raise. The total amount might include past-due payments, late fees, attorney's fees and any other costs associated with the default.

Here are things that you can liquidate to provide cash to cure the default:
- Cars (with or without loans)
- RVs/Motorhomes (with or without loans)
- Second Homes (with or without loans)
- Precious Metals (silver, gold, etc.)
- Jewelry
- Life insurance policy

If you have any of the first 4 things on the list that you want to liquidate for cash quickly, send me a text at (423) 460-6111 with the following information (text only for this service, please):
- Let me know you're trying to come up with funds to pay off past-due property taxes so that I know what the goal is
- Let me know what exactly you have and what kind of condition it's in

And I may buy those things from you or know someone that will. Keep in mind that I or my referrals can't pay retail value.

If you're thinking about selling your property, visit page 118 so that you can hear how I might be able to make that a smooth process for you.

If this solution didn't help or you think it won't work for you, return back to the Delinquent Property Tax Flowchart on page 46.

Unpaid Property Taxes: File for Chapter 7 Bankruptcy

In some cases, having delinquent property taxes may be accompanied by financial challenges that may require you to consider bankruptcy as an option.

Bankruptcy attorneys can provide legal advice and representation in bankruptcy proceedings. They can help you understand the different types of bankruptcy, assess your eligibility, and navigate the complex legal process.

Bankruptcy can have a significant impact on your financial situation, and it's important to seek professional legal advice before making any decisions.

Filing for bankruptcy because of delinquent property taxes can have both positive and negative consequences, depending on your specific circumstances.

Positives of Filing for Bankruptcy with past due property taxes:

1. *Automatic Stay*: One of the main benefits of filing for bankruptcy is that it triggers an automatic stay, which is a legal order that halts all collection actions, including tax sale proceedings. This can provide immediate relief to you by stopping the tax sale process and giving you time to assess your financial situation and explore potential options to save your property.

2. *Discharge of Debts*: Chapter 7 bankruptcy allows for the discharge of certain unsecured debts, such as credit card debt, medical bills, and personal loans. This can free up your financial resources and help you focus on resolving your property tax delinquency and catching up on overdue payments. Mortgage debts are also eligible to be discharged. Sometimes, property taxes older than 1 year are also eligible to be discharged. Tax liens, on the other hand, can never be discharged through bankruptcy. So if your unpaid property taxes have been converted into a tax lien that will stay in place no matter what.

3. *Protection of Other Assets*: Bankruptcy can also provide protection for other assets, such as personal property or savings accounts, from being seized by creditors. This can help you retain some financial stability during the tax sale process and potentially safeguard your other assets from being liquidated.

4. *Fresh Start*: Chapter 7 bankruptcy is often referred to as a "fresh start" bankruptcy because it allows you to eliminate or reduce your debt burden, giving you a chance to rebuild your financial future without the weight of unmanageable debts.

Negatives of Filing for Bankruptcy with Past Due Property Taxes:

1. *Impact on Credit*: Filing for Chapter 7 bankruptcy will have a negative impact on your credit score and will remain on your credit report for up to 10 years. This can make it more challenging to obtain credit in the future and may affect your ability to secure loans, rent a home, or even find employment.

2. *Tax Sale Still Possible*: While the automatic stay can temporarily halt tax sale proceedings, it's important to note that Chapter 7 bankruptcy does not guarantee that you will be able to keep your property. If you are significantly behind on your property tax payments and unable to catch up during the bankruptcy process, the lender may seek relief from the automatic stay and proceed with the tax sale.

3. *Legal and Filing Fees*: Filing for bankruptcy involves various legal and filing fees, which can add to the financial burden you're already facing. These fees can vary depending on the type of bankruptcy filed and the complexity of the case, and may need to be paid upfront.

4. *Loss of Non-exempt Assets*: Chapter 7 bankruptcy involves liquidating non-exempt assets to repay creditors. If you have valuable assets that are not protected by bankruptcy exemptions, they may be sold to repay your debts, including your property taxes. This could potentially result in the loss of property, including your home, if it is not protected by exemptions.

5. *Public Record*: Bankruptcy filings are public records, which means that your financial situation and bankruptcy status may become a matter of public record. This lack of privacy can be a disadvantage if you wish to keep your financial situation confidential.

It's important to note that bankruptcy laws and procedures can be complex and vary by jurisdiction. Therefore, it's crucial to consult with a qualified bankruptcy attorney who can assess your individual financial situation, explain the potential consequences of filing for Chapter 7 bankruptcy with delinquent taxes, and help you navigate the bankruptcy process effectively.

Additionally, it's important to consider all available options, including alternatives to bankruptcy, and weigh the pros and cons before making a decision.

Attorneys can be sharks (and not always in the best way). If you'd like a referral to a trusted and proven Bankruptcy Attorney in my network, send me a text to (423) 460-6111 and let me know. (please, text only for this service)

If you choose Chapter 7 Bankruptcy, you may have to sell your property. If you do, visit page 118 so that you can hear how I might be able to make that a smooth process for you and get the Bankruptcy over with quicker.

If this solution didn't help or you think it won't work for you, return back to the Delinquent Property Tax Flowchart on page 46.

Unpaid Property Taxes: Filing for Chapter 13 Bankruptcy

Filing for Chapter 13 bankruptcy with past due property taxes can have both positives and negatives, and it's crucial to carefully evaluate your financial situation and consult with a qualified bankruptcy attorney before making any decisions.

Positives of filing Chapter 13 bankruptcy with unpaid property taxes:

1. *Automatic Stay*: Filing for Chapter 13 bankruptcy triggers an automatic stay, which temporarily halts tax sale proceedings. This provides you with immediate relief from the stress of a tax sale and an opportunity to figure out how to bring your property taxes current.
2. *Repayment Plan*: Chapter 13 bankruptcy allows you to propose a repayment plan to catch up on your property tax arrears over a period of three to five years. This can provide you with a structured and manageable plan to repay your past-due property taxes while keeping your property.
3. *Protecting Your Assets*: Chapter 13 bankruptcy allows you to retain ownership and possession of your assets, including your property, while you work on repaying your debts through the court-approved repayment plan. This can provide you with the opportunity to save your property from tax sale and keep your other assets as well.
4. *Debt Consolidation*: Chapter 13 bankruptcy consolidates your debts into a single repayment plan, which can make it more manageable to repay your creditors, including your property taxes. This can help you regain control of your finances and create a plan to catch up on your property taxes and other debts over time.
5. *Improved Credit Standing*: Chapter 13 bankruptcy will have a negative impact on your credit score and typically remains on your credit report for seven years. But as you make regular payments under the court-approved repayment plan, it may help improve your credit standing over time.

Negatives of filing Chapter 13 bankruptcy during foreclosure:

1. *Repayment Plan Requirements*: Filing for Chapter 13 bankruptcy requires you to propose a court-approved repayment plan and make regular payments over a period of three to five years. This may require significant financial discipline and may limit your discretionary spending during the repayment period. If you are unable to make the required monthly payments, your bankruptcy case may be dismissed, and the tax sale process may resume.

2. *Lengthy Process*: Chapter 13 bankruptcy is a long-term commitment, typically lasting three to five years, during which you are required to make regular payments under the court-approved repayment plan. This can be a significant time commitment and may require you to adhere to a strict budget and financial plan for an extended period.

3. *Impact on Credit*: Filing Chapter 13 bankruptcy will have a negative impact on your credit score, and it will remain on your credit report for 7 years. This may affect your ability to obtain credit in the future, including loans, credit cards, and other forms of credit.

4. *Public Record*: Chapter 13 bankruptcy is a public record, and your filing will be recorded in public records accessible to the public, which may impact your privacy and financial reputation.

It's important to note that bankruptcy laws and procedures can be complex and vary by jurisdiction. Therefore, it's crucial to consult with a qualified bankruptcy attorney who can assess your individual financial situation, explain the potential consequences of filing for Chapter 13 bankruptcy while being behind on property taxes, and help you navigate the bankruptcy process effectively.

Additionally, it's important to consider all available options, including alternatives to bankruptcy, and weigh the pros and cons before making a decision.

Attorneys can be sharks (and not always in the best way). If you'd like a referral to a trusted and proven Bankruptcy Attorney in my network, send me a text to (423) 460-6111 and let me know. (please, text only for this service)

If you choose Chapter 7 Bankruptcy, you may have to sell your property. If you do, visit page 118 so that you can hear how I might be able to make that a smooth process for you and get the Bankruptcy over with quicker.

If this solution didn't help or you think it won't work for you, return back to the Delinquent Property Tax Flowchart on page 46.

Unpaid Property Taxes: Tax Deferral

If you are behind on your property taxes, you might be able to apply for a tax deferral. Some local governments offer tax deferral programs that allow you to delay paying your property taxes until a later date.

These programs are typically reserved for senior citizens or people with disabilities. Contact your local tax collector's office to see if you qualify for a tax deferral.

It's important to take action as soon as possible if you are behind on your property taxes. Ignoring the problem can lead to additional fees, penalties, and even a tax sale. Ignoring the problem also causes you lose some options available to you.

Talking to the government can be scary. I offer a service where I will talk to your county, explain your situation and gather the options they are willing to do and present them to you. It's only $97 and well worth it. If this interests you, give me a call at (423) 460-6111 right now (day or night). If I don't answer, please leave a message so I know you called.

If you're thinking about selling your property, visit page 118 so that you can hear how I might be able to make that a smooth process for you.

If this solution didn't help or you think it won't work for you, return back to the Delinquent Property Tax Flowchart on page 46.

Unpaid Property Taxes: Doing Nothing

There's very little advice that I can give with 100% certainty without knowing your specific situation. But this is one of those pieces of advice that applies to everyone: DOING NOTHING IS THE WORST THING YOU CAN DO.

If you do nothing, you get the full force of the tax sale process and there's no way to soften any blows.

If the tax sale completes on your property, it means that the county (or other person that bought your taxes) has taken legal action to enforce their right to seize and sell your property due to your default on the property taxes. The specific process and consequences of a tax sale can vary depending on the laws and regulations of your state or jurisdiction.

However, in general, the following may happen if the tax sale on your property completes and you don't do anything:

1. *Loss of Ownership*: The most significant consequence of a tax sale is the loss of ownership of your property. Once the tax sale process is completed, the county or person that bought your taxes bank becomes the legal owner of the property, and you are required to vacate the premises.
2. *Eviction*: If you do not voluntarily vacate the property after the tax sale, the county or person that bought your taxes may initiate eviction proceedings to legally remove you from the property. Eviction is a legal process that typically involves court proceedings and can result in the involvement of law enforcement to forcibly remove you from the property.

3. *Loss of Equity*: If you have built up equity in your property, which is the difference between the market value of the property and the remaining mortgage balance, a tax sale may result in the loss of that equity. The property is typically sold at a tax sale or other means, and the proceeds are used to satisfy the outstanding property taxes, legal fees, and other costs associated with the tax sale process. If the proceeds are not enough to cover the debt, you may lose your equity in the property.

4. *Emotional and Psychological Impact*: Going through a tax sale can also have emotional and psychological impacts. Losing your property, facing eviction, and dealing with the financial and legal consequences of a tax sale can be stressful, emotionally draining, and may impact your overall well-being and quality of life.

If you're thinking about selling your property, visit page 118 so that you can hear how I might be able to make that a smooth process for you.

If you now understand why doing nothing isn't really an option (and I hope you do), return back to the Delinquent Property Tax Flowchart on page 46 to see what your course of action should be.

I Need to Relocate

Overall, selling a property when you need to relocate by a certain date can be challenging, but with the right strategy and mindset, it is achievable.

When you need to relocate, you typically have to do it within a short time frame because:
1. you need to be in your new place/city by a specific date
2. you don't want to end up with 2 house payments

The short time frame usually eliminates selling for sale by owner (FSBO) or with an agent because the timelines with those selling methods are unpredictable.

It typically takes at least 45 days to sell with an agent (and that's assuming everything runs as it should). But if your buyer's financing ends up falling through at the last minute, the clock starts over again. So it could take months to sell the traditional way.

And selling for sale by owner (FSBO) takes even longer because you don't have access to as large of a buyer pool as an agent would.

Sometimes, folks leave renting their old place on the table. I would highly advise against that. The landlord horror stories you usually hear about typically come from folks that became what I call "accidental landlords." Meaning they didn't want to be landlords but it was something they fell into.

Being a landlord isn't something you just want to stumble into. It takes years of experience to become a successful landlord. It's no walk in the park and it's filled with landmines. And managing a property from another city is a challenge in and of itself.

When you're on a timeline, you need to be flexible with your price and/or terms. **The best way to sell a property when you need to relocate is by selling to an iBuyer. Read more about it on page 118.**

I Have Filed/I'm Going to File Bankruptcy

In bankruptcy, the fate of your property depends on the type of bankruptcy you file, the value of your property, and the exemptions you're eligible for.

In Chapter 7 bankruptcy, a trustee may be appointed to liquidate any non-exempt assets to pay off your creditors. Exempt assets are those that are protected by law, and you are allowed to keep them.

Each state has different exemptions, so it's important to consult a bankruptcy attorney in your area to understand what assets are exempt in your state.

In Chapter 13 bankruptcy, you typically don't have to sell any property, but you'll need to pay off your debts over a 3-5 year period through a court-approved repayment plan. Your assets may affect the amount of your monthly payment.

Here are some general steps to follow:

Consult with your bankruptcy attorney: Overall, bankruptcy is a complex legal process, and it's essential to consult a bankruptcy attorney to understand how your property will be affected in bankruptcy and what options are available to you. Your attorney will also be able to determine how your property will be affected by the bankruptcy case and any potential exemptions.

Determine the equity in the property: Equity is the difference between the value of the property and the amount owed on any mortgages or liens. If there is equity in the property, it may be subject to seizure by the bankruptcy trustee to pay off creditors.

If you choose to sell your property: If you want to sell your property, you will need to obtain permission from the bankruptcy court. In Chapter 7 bankruptcy, you will need to obtain permission from the bankruptcy court to sell the property. In Chapter 13 bankruptcy, you may need to modify your repayment plan to reflect the sale of the property. Once you have obtained permission from the bankruptcy court, you'll have to find a buyer (more on this in a second). It's important to note that any proceeds from the sale will be subject to the bankruptcy court's approval and may be used to pay off creditors.

Bankruptcy can be a complex process, and it's important to work closely with your bankruptcy attorney to ensure that you comply with all requirements and procedures.

Attorneys can be sharks (and not always in the best way). If you'd like a referral to a trusted and proven Bankruptcy Attorney in my network, send me a text to (423) 460-6111 and let me know. (please, text only for this service)

If you choose Bankruptcy, you may have to sell your property. If you do, visit page 118 so that you can hear how I might be able to make that a smooth process for you and get the Bankruptcy over with quicker.

I'm Going to File/I'm Going Through a Divorce

In a divorce, the division of property is typically decided through a legal process. The fate of the property will depend on several factors such as the state laws and the couple's specific circumstances, including who owns the property, whether it was purchased before or after the marriage, and whether it was acquired through inheritance or a gift.

In general, the property may be sold and the proceeds divided between the spouses, or one spouse may be awarded the property and may be required to buy out the other spouse's share of the equity. Alternatively, the couple may choose to continue co-owning the property.

It's important to consult with a qualified divorce attorney to understand your specific legal rights and options when it comes to the division of property, including your house, in a divorce.

Attorneys can be sharks (and not always in a good way). If you'd like a referral to a trusted and proven Divorce Attorney in my network, send me a text to (423) 460-6111 and let me know. (please, text only for this service)

If you get divorced, you may have to (or may choose to) sell your property. If you do, visit page 118 so that you can hear how I might be able to make that a smooth process for you and get the divorce completed a lot quicker for you.

If you have (or will have) a partial interest in a piece of property with your ex-partner and want to sell it, I can also explore buying that partial interest. Go to page 69 for more details.

I Have a Partial Interest in a Property that I Want to Sell

A partial interest in real estate means that you own a percentage of a property. Maybe you own 50% of a property and your ex-partner owns the other 50% of the property.

Selling a partial interest in real estate involves selling a portion of the ownership of a property, while someone else retains their share of ownership.

You could want to sell your interest for any number of reasons. Maybe you have no interest in sharing in the property expenses anymore. Or maybe the property just doesn't have any equity. Or maybe you just don't get along with the other owner anymore.

If the property is jointly owned with other individuals, you will need to review the ownership agreement to see if you have the right to sell your partial interest.

Very few buyers are interested in purchasing a partial interest in a property, which makes them very hard to sell. So any traditional selling methods are out.

An iBuyer is probably your only possibility. You should be aware that you're not going to get market value for your interest because only buying a partial interest in a property usually brings a lot of problems (those problems might even be the reason why you're trying to sell your interest). So you should be prepared to sell at a discount.

If you're thinking about selling your partial interest, visit page 118 so that you can hear how I might be able to make that a smooth process for you.

I'm Paying for 2 Properties and It's Straining Me

Having 2 house payments can be very stressful as it depletes your bank account. As fast as money comes in, it seems to go out even faster.

Maybe you got in this situation because you had to relocate fast and thought you could sell your old property quicker. Or maybe you saw your dream house and just had to have it before selling your old house. Whatever the reason, it can cause a lot of stress.

And if you fall behind on a payment, it can wreak havoc on your credit and financial situation.

For most folks, listing with an agent or trying to sell for sale by owner (FSBO) just isn't going to alleviate the problem fast enough.

Selling with an agent takes a minimum of 45 days (and that's if everything goes perfectly). If your buyer's financing falls through at the last minute it could reset the clock and you'll have to start all over again. Then you're looking at it taking months to sell.

Selling to an iBuyer is going to be the best route most of the time. Visit page 118 to find out more. You could have your property under contract TODAY and get financial relief in as soon as a few days.

A Minor Wants to Sell Their Interest in a Property

In general, minors (individuals under the age of 18 in most jurisdictions) are not legally able to enter into contracts and may not be able to sell their interest in a property without the consent of their legal guardian or a court-appointed representative. This is because minors are considered to lack the legal capacity to enter into binding contracts.

If a minor wishes to sell their interest in a property, they will need to work with their legal guardian or court-appointed representative to navigate the legal requirements.

Depending on the jurisdiction, this may involve obtaining court approval, appointing a legal guardian to act on behalf of the minor, or taking other steps to ensure that the sale is legally valid.

It's important to note that laws regarding minors and property transactions can vary widely depending on the jurisdiction.

Because of the complex nature of a transaction with a minor, 99%+ of buyers wouldn't be interested in the transaction, so selling with an agent or for sale by owner (FSBO) usually isn't a good option.

Selling to an iBuyer is usually your best option in this situation because they have experience with this kind of transaction. Visit page 118 for more information.

If the minor is looking to sell a partial interest in a property, refer to page 69.

I Inherited a Property and Don't Know What to Do

Inheriting a property can sometimes be a blessing and a curse. It's a blessing because it's an asset and has the potential to improve your financial situation. And it's a curse because it often brings some difficult and complicated decisions (often unexpectedly).

When inheriting a property WITHOUT a will, the laws of the state where the property is located will determine who inherits the property. If the property was passed on to you through intestate succession (without a will), you will need to follow the legal process to establish your ownership.

Inheriting a property WITH a will (that is recent) will typically require the property to go through a process called probate.

Probate is the legal process that occurs after someone passes away. It is the court-supervised process of identifying and gathering the assets of the deceased person, paying any debts or taxes owed by the estate, and distributing the remaining assets to the rightful heirs or beneficiaries.

If there is a will that is older than that and it didn't go through probate (or if it's a smaller estate), you might be able to go through a faster process that is used if there wasn't a will at all. That's outside of the scope of this chapter. We'll just be covering probate here because that's the most common.

Here's a general overview of the probate process:

Determine if you are the legal heir: If the person who owned the property has passed away, the first step is to determine if you are the legal heir. This usually depends on whether the deceased person had a will, and if so, whether you were named as a beneficiary. If there is no will, you need to figure out if you would be next in line to inherit the property, according to the family tree of the deceased..

Obtain a death certificate: You will need to obtain a copy of the deceased person's death certificate to prove that they have passed away.

File a petition for probate: If there is a will, the executor named in the will must file a petition for probate in court. This is a legal process that establishes the validity of the will and appoints the executor to manage the deceased person's estate.

Notifying heirs and creditors: All heirs and creditors are notified of the probate proceedings and given an opportunity to contest any claims against the estate.

Inventory the assets: The executor must create an inventory of all the deceased person's assets, including real estate, bank accounts, investments, and personal property.

Pay any debts: Before any assets can be distributed to heirs or beneficiaries, the executor must use the estate's assets to pay any outstanding debts or taxes owed by the deceased person.

Distributing assets: Once all debts and taxes have been paid, the remaining assets are distributed to the heirs or beneficiaries according to the deceased person's will or the laws of intestacy if there is no will.

The probate process can be lengthy and complex, depending on the size and complexity of the estate. However, it is an important legal process that ensures that the deceased person's assets are distributed fairly and according to their wishes.

The specific details of the inheritance process can vary depending on the jurisdiction and the circumstances of the inheritance.

Most people choose to sell an inherited property because they usually already have a place to live. And sometimes selling an inherited property can be a complex process, especially if there are multiple heirs involved or if the property is located in a different state or country.

A lot of times, inherited properties aren't in modern shape because someone elderly lived there and they didn't feel the need to update it. Selling a property that isn't modern is very difficult through normal channels. When selling on the open market, most buyers want a property that is ready to move-in to.

This usually leaves selling to an iBuyer being your only option because they specifically look for properties that they can buy and add value to to create a profit for themselves.

If you're thinking about selling your inherited property (or a property you will inherit), visit page 118 so that you can hear how I might be able to make that a smooth process for you.

If you need (or are going to need) an Estate Sale Company to help you sell the valuables of the estate or clean out the house, send me a text to (423) 460-6111 to get a referral. (please, text only for this service).

I Have a Property with Breaks in the Title Chain

A break in the title chain refers to a missing or incomplete record of ownership of a property. This can occur if there is a gap in the ownership history of the property, such as if a previous owner did not properly transfer the property to the next owner. It can also occur if there was an error in the recording of the ownership transfer. Or a missing deed.

A break in the title chain can create legal and financial issues for the current owner of the property, as it can prevent them from selling or refinancing the property until the ownership history is properly established and recorded.

To fix a break in the title chain, you have 2 options:

1. *Hire a real estate attorney to do it for you.* The attorney will conduct a title search and investigate the ownership history of the property. If there are any missing or incomplete records, the attorney will need to work to locate the missing information and correct any errors or omissions in the ownership records. Once the ownership history of the property is properly established, the title company can issue a clear title to the current owner, which will allow them to sell or refinance the property without any legal or financial issues arising from the break in the title chain. Keep in mind that this option runs, on average, about $15k in legal fees (obviously, it depends on how complex the break in title is… it could be more or less). It also typically takes 6 to 12 months to fix.

2. *You can sell the property as-is to an iBuyer.* When you sell to an iBuyer, you wouldn't have to fix the title (the iBuyer would take care of that after they bought it). You would need to be flexible on price and terms and you would have to sell the property for significantly less than retail because title issues are risky (and some title issues just can't be fixed). Selling a property with title issues with an agent or for sale by owner (FSBO) just isn't an option because 99.9% of people won't be interested in a property with title issues.

Attorneys can be sharks (and not always in the best way). If you'd like a referral to a trusted and proven Real Estate Attorney in my network, send me a text to (423) 460-6111 and let me know. (please, texts only for this service)

If you'd like to sell your property with title issues as-is visit page 118 for more details and learn how I can make the process easy and painless for you.

I Have a Property with a Fraudulent/Forged Deed in the Chain of Title

When fraud or forgery occurs with a deed, it can have serious legal consequences. A deed is a legal document that establishes ownership of a property, and any fraudulent or forged deed can lead to the transfer of ownership of a property to someone who has no legal right to it.

If you suspect that a deed has been fraudulently or forged, you have 2 options:

1. *Contact a real estate attorney.* They can help you investigate the matter and take the necessary legal action to protect your rights. In some cases, the legal process may involve a lawsuit to void the fraudulent or forged deed and restore the rightful owner's ownership of the property. Additionally, the individuals responsible for the fraud or forgery may face criminal charges. It is important to note that the laws and legal procedures surrounding fraud and forgery of deeds can vary depending on the jurisdiction. Keep in mind that this option runs, on average, about $15k in legal fees (obviously, it depends on how complex the issue is… it could be more or less). It also typically takes 6 to 12 months to fix.

2. *You can sell the property as-is to an iBuyer.* You wouldn't have to fix the title (the iBuyer would take care of that after they bought it). You would need to be flexible on price and terms and you will have to sell the property for significantly less than retail because buying properties with fraudulent title issues is risky. Selling a property with a forged/fraudulent deed with an agent or for sale by owner (FSBO) just isn't an option because 99.9% of people won't be interested in a property with those issues.

Attorneys can be sharks (and not always in the best way). If you'd like a referral to a trusted and proven Real Estate Attorney in my network, send me a text to (423) 460-6111 and let me know. (please, text only for this service)

If you'd like to sell your property as-is (without fixing the deed/title issues) visit page 118 for more details and learn how I can make the process easy and painless for you.

There is an Invalid Power of Attorney in the Title Chain

When a property is sold with an invalid power of attorney, the sale may be considered void or unenforceable. This means that the sale may be invalidated and the property may be returned to its original owner.

The validity of a power of attorney is determined by various factors, including whether the document was executed properly and whether the agent had the authority to act on behalf of the principal. If the power of attorney was not executed properly or if the agent did not have the authority to act, then any transaction entered into using that power of attorney may be considered invalid.

If you suspect that a property has been sold with an invalid power of attorney, you have 2 options:

1. *Contact a real estate attorney.* They can help you investigate the matter and take the necessary legal action to protect your rights. If a property was sold with an invalid power of attorney, the original owner may need to take legal action to have the sale invalidated and the property returned to them. This may involve filing a lawsuit or taking other legal steps to challenge the sale. Keep in mind that this option runs, on average, about $15k in legal fees (obviously, it depends on how complex the issue is… it could be more or less). It also typically takes 6 to 12 months to fix.
2. *You can sell the property as-is to an iBuyer.* You wouldn't have to fix the title (the iBuyer would take care of that after they bought it). You would need to be flexible on price and terms and you will have to sell the property for significantly less than retail because buying properties with title issues like this is risky. Selling a property that has title issues with an agent or for sale by owner just isn't an option because 99.9% of people won't be interested in a property with those issues.

Attorneys can be sharks (and not always in a good way). If you'd like a referral to a trusted and proven Real Estate Attorney in my network, send me a text to (423) 460-6111 and let me know. (please, text only for this service)

If you'd like to sell your property as-is (without fixing the power of attorney issue) visit page 118 for more details and learn how I can make the process easy and painless for you.

I Inherited a Property and Some Heirs Are Missing

Finding missing heirs that have moved onto other cities or other countries can be difficult. Sometimes past family squabbles leave missing heirs not wanting to be found.

If you cannot find the heirs for a property, there are a 2 options you have:

1. *Contact a probate attorney.* A probate attorney can help you navigate the legal process of identifying and locating heirs. They can also assist with filing a petition to appoint an administrator for the estate if necessary. Keep in mind that this option runs, on average, about $15k in legal fees (obviously, it depends on how complex the estate is… it could be more or less). It also typically takes 5 to 8 months to complete.
2. *You can sell the property as-is to an iBuyer.* You would need to be flexible on price and terms and you would may even have to sell the property for significantly less than retail because buying properties with missing heirs is risky. Selling a property with an unclear title with an agent or for sale by owner (FSBO) just isn't an option because 99.9% of people won't be interested in a property with those issues.

Attorneys can be sharks (and not always in a good way). If you'd like a referral to a trusted and proven Probate Attorney in my network, send me a text to (423) 460-6111 and let me know. (please, text only for this service)

If you'd like to sell your property as-is (without fixing the issue of missing heirs) visit page 118 for more details and learn how I can make the process easy and painless.

A Will Was Discovered After the Sale of the Property

If a will is discovered after a property is sold, the situation can become complicated. The effect of the will on the sale of the property will depend on several factors, including the nature of the property and the terms of the will.

If the property was sold before the will was discovered and the new owner had no knowledge of the will, the sale of the property will generally stand.

However, if the will specifically bequeaths the property to someone else, that person may have a claim against the estate or the proceeds of the sale.

If the property was sold after the will was discovered, the executor of the estate may have the power to rescind the sale if it was not authorized by the terms of the will. This will depend on the specific language of the will and the laws of the state in which the property is located.

In any case, it is important to consult with an experienced attorney who can help determine the legal rights and obligations of all parties involved.

Attorneys can be sharks (and not always in a good way). If you'd like a referral to a trusted and proven Probate Attorney in my network, send me a text to (423) 460-6111 and let me know. (please, text only for this service)

If you are the one that ends up with ownership of the property after the dust settles and you'd like to sell your property as-is, visit page 118 for more details and learn how I can make the process easy and painless for you.

There is a Boundary Dispute/Encroachment

A property boundary dispute occurs when two or more parties disagree on the location of a property line. This can happen for various reasons, such as an unclear or outdated property survey, a misunderstanding about the property's legal description, or a neighbor building a fence or structure that encroaches on the other's property.

If there is a property boundary dispute, the parties involved should try to resolve it amicably. This may involve reviewing property surveys, obtaining legal advice, or negotiating a compromise. If the parties cannot resolve the dispute on their own, they may need to involve a mediator or go to court.

In court, a judge may consider various factors to determine the true boundary line, such as the language of the property deed, the location of physical features such as trees or fences, and the testimony of witnesses. The court may also consider factors such as the parties' use of the disputed land and the degree of harm caused by one party's encroachment on the other's property.

Ultimately, the outcome of a property boundary dispute will depend on the specific circumstances of the case and the legal principles involved. It is important for anyone facing a property boundary dispute to seek legal advice and representation to ensure their rights are protected and their interests are safeguarded.

Attorneys can be sharks (and not always in a good way). If you'd like a referral to a trusted and proven Real Estate Attorney in my network, send me a text to (423) 460-6111 and let me know. (please, text only for this service)

If you'd like to sell your property (without fixing the boundary dispute issue) visit page 118 for more details and learn how I can make the process easy and painless for you.

There Is No Easement (Landlocked Property)

When a property is landlocked, it means that the property has no direct access to a public road, right-of-way or easement. This can make the property difficult to access and may limit its potential uses.

An easement is a legal right that allows one party to use another party's land for a specific purpose, such as accessing a public road, installing utility lines, or crossing a property to reach a nearby parcel.

Disputes can happen with easements too. An easement dispute can occur when there is a disagreement between two or more parties regarding the rights and responsibilities associated with an easement.

If there is no clear easement to your property, there are a 2 options you have:

1. *Contact a real estate attorney.* An attorney can help you analyze your options. An attorney can possibly help you negotiate an easement or right-of-way with the neighboring property owner(s) in order to gain access to the public road. If the neighboring property owner(s) are unwilling to grant an easement, the landlocked property owner may need to take legal action to establish their right to access the public road. In some cases, the government may also become involved to ensure that the landlocked property owner has reasonable access to their property. Keep in mind that this option runs, on average, about $15k in legal fees (obviously, it depends on how complex the issue is… it could be more or less). That DOESN'T include the cost of the easement you might need to buy from an adjacent landowner. It also typically takes 5 to 8 months to complete.

2. *You can sell the property as-is to an iBuyer.* You would need to be flexible on price and terms and you would may even have to sell the property for significantly less than retail because buying properties with no access is risky. Selling a property with no access with an agent or for sale by owner (FSBO) just isn't an option because 99.9% of people won't be interested in a property with those issues.

Attorneys can be sharks (and not always in a good way). If you'd like a referral to a trusted and proven Real Estate Attorney in my network, send me a text to (423) 460-6111 and let me know. (please, text only for this service)

If you'd like to sell your property as-is (without fixing the easement issue) visit page 118 for more details and learn how I can make the process easy and painless for you.

I Want to Sell BUT ____ (Insert Reason)…

This chapter is the catch-all chapter.

Maybe you've been trying to sell your property but it's not selling for some reason.

Maybe you've been wanting to sell but feel that you can't for some reason or that nobody would be interested in buying into a negative situation that you have going on with the property.

Whatever the reason, an iBuyer might be able to help. They buy properties that the general market won't touch.

They may not be able to offer you full market value but they can help you accomplish your goal of selling the property.

If you'd like to sell your property as-is (with whatever issue it has) visit page 118 for more details and learn how I can make the process easy and painless for you.

My Property Won't Sell/Has Been on the Market Awhile

I'm sorry to hear that you're having trouble selling your property. There are many factors that can contribute to difficulty selling a property, such as the current state of the real estate market, the condition of the property, and its location.

Here are some potential reasons why you might be having difficulty selling your property:

Your asking price is too high: The price you're asking for your property might be higher than what the market is willing to pay, and buyers may be hesitant to make an offer.

Your property is in poor condition: If your property is in poor condition, buyers may be turned off by the amount of work that needs to be done and may be hesitant to purchase it.

Your property is in an undesirable location: The location of your property may not be desirable to buyers, which can make it more difficult to sell.

Your marketing strategy isn't effective: If you're not using effective marketing strategies to promote your property, you may not be reaching the right audience and potential buyers may not be aware that your property is for sale.

Here are a few steps you can take to potentially improve your chances of selling your property:

1. *Use an Agent*: If you have a property that is updated and move-in ready and you don't have to sell soon and you don't mind paying a 6% commission (which is $24,000 on the median property price of $400,000), this option is probably for you. **If you'd like a referral to a top agent, send me a text to (423) 460-6111. (please, text only for this service)**

2. *Sell to an iBuyer*: If you want your property sold now (and as-is) and don't want to pay commissions or closing costs, and you don't want to take on the issues of rectifying whatever is causing buyers not to be interested in your property, consider selling to an iBuyer. An iBuyer can close on the date of your choice and make everything easy. **See page 118 for more information.**

My Property Needs Repairs/a Rehab

Selling a property that needs repairs can be a bit challenging because almost all agent and for sale by owner (FSBO) buyer pools are looking for move-in ready properties.

So there are typically 2 options available to you:

Make the repairs and list with an agent: If you don't have the money for the repairs, you can apply for a home improvement loan or a personal loan to cover the cost of repairs. Once the repairs are complete, you can list the property with an agent and fetch the full retail price. I can always refer you to a trusted and proven contractor if you need help making the repairs (see below).

Sell for sale by owner (FSBO): If you are pretty familiar with real estate, marketing, staging, etc., then this option may be for you. If you don't have a lot of confidence in your real estate game, I would avoid this option.

Sell the property "as is" to an iBuyer: One option is to sell the property to an iBuyer in its current condition without making any repairs. You should still be transparent about the issues with the property to stay out of legal trouble. iBuyers are are often willing to buy properties that need repairs for a discount because they can fix them up and resell them for a profit. They can also close quickly, which can be beneficial if you need to sell your property quickly. **See page 118 for more information on how an iBuyer can help you.**

Just so you're aware, this is the universal iBuyer formula on a property that needs repairs. Let's say that the After Repair Value (ARV) of the property is $200,000. This is the retail value of the property IF it were fully fixed up. This isn't a number that you're entitled to or to benefit from unless YOU do the repairs but it's a number that an iBuyer takes into account. And let's say the property needs $40,000 in repairs to bring it up to that $200,000 value. To calculate your offer price, they would take $200,000 and multiply it by 65% (you would get $130,000) and then subtract the repairs ($40,000) and offer you $90,000.

It may seem like a low offer but there's a lot of risk in renovating a property. And the iBuyer has to pay 2 sets of closing costs (one to buy the property and one to sell it).

If you'd like to sell your property as-is visit page 118 for more details and learn how I can make the process easy and painless for you.

If you'd like a referral to a trusted and proven contractor, send me a text to (423) 460-6111 (please, text only for this service).

My Property Has Damage from a Fire or Natural Disaster

It's very unfortunate when a fire or natural disaster destroys all or part of a property you worked so hard for.

Sometimes even if you have insurance, you might be in charge of liquidating what's left of the property after an insurance settlement. These properties are hard to sell (and sell for a big discount) because unseen damage can lurk behind the walls and under the floors that can't be easily seen with an inspection.

For instance, if you had a fire… there can be a lot of smoke and water damage to the rest of the house even if the fire was put out quickly and the obvious fire damage itself was limited to just 1 room of the property.

So these are typically your 3 options available to you:

Make the repairs and list with an agent: If you don't have the money for the repairs, you can apply for a home improvement loan or a personal loan to cover the cost of repairs. Once the repairs are complete, you can list the property with an agent and fetch the full retail price. If you need a referral to a contractor, please see below.

Sell the property for sale by owner (FSBO): Unless you have a decent amount of real estate experience, I don't recommend this for the average property seller. **But if you wish to explore this option, please see page 110 for more information.**

Sell the property "as is" to an iBuyer: One option is to sell the property to an iBuyer in its current condition without making any repairs. You should still be transparent about its condition to stay out of legal trouble. iBuyers are are often willing to buy properties that need repairs for a discount because they can fix them up and resell them for a profit. They can also close quickly, which can be beneficial if you need to sell your property quickly. **See page 118 for more information.**

Just so you're aware, this is the universal iBuyer formula on a property that needs repairs. Let's say that the After Repair Value (ARV) of the property is $200,000. This is the retail value of the property IF it were fully fixed up. This isn't a number that you're entitled to or to benefit from unless YOU do the repairs but it's a number that an iBuyer takes into account.. And let's say the property needs $40,000 in repairs to bring it up to that $200,000 value. To calculate your offer price, they would take $200,000 and multiply it by 65% (you would get $130,000) and then subtract the repairs ($40,000) and offer you $90,000.

It may seem like a low offer but there's a lot of risk in renovating a property. And the iBuyer has to pay 2 sets of closing costs (one to buy the property and one to sell it).

If you'd like to sell your property as-is visit page 118 for more details and learn how I can make the process easy and painless for you.

If you'd like a referral to a trusted and proven contractor or agent, send me a text to (423) 460-6111 (please, text only for this service).

My Property Didn't Pass Inspection

I'm sorry to hear that your house didn't pass inspection. This could be the buyer's home inspection or the point of sale inspection required by your local municipality.

You really have 2 options in this situation:

1. *Fix the Problems Yourself and Sell How You Were Going to Sell*: Get a copy of the inspection report and review it carefully. Make note of any repairs or improvements that need to be made. Make the necessary repairs or improvements. This may include fixing any electrical or plumbing issues, addressing structural problems or making cosmetic upgrades. If you don't have the money to make the repairs, you could try applying for a home equity or home improvement loan or even check with your local bank to see if you can get a personal loan. I can refer you to a trusted and proven contractor if you need it (please see below).

2. *Sell the property "as is" to an iBuyer*: One option is to sell the property to an iBuyer in its current condition without making any repairs. You should still be transparent about the condition of the property to stay out of legal trouble. iBuyers are are often willing to buy properties that need repairs for a discount because they can fix them up and resell them for a profit. They can also close quickly, which can be beneficial if you need to sell your property quickly. **See page 118 for more information on how to work with an iBuyer.**

Just so you're aware, this is the universal iBuyer formula on a property that needs repairs. Let's say that the After Repair Value (ARV) of the property is $200,000. This is the retail value of the property IF it were fully fixed up. This isn't a number that you're entitled to or to benefit from unless YOU do the repairs but it's a number that an iBuyer takes into account. And let's say the property needs $40,000 in repairs to bring it up to that $200,000 value. To calculate your offer price, they would take $200,000 and multiply it by 65% (you would get $130,000) and then subtract the repairs ($40,000) and offer you $90,000.

It may seem like a low offer but there's a lot of risk in renovating a property. And the iBuyer has to pay 2 sets of closing costs (one to buy the property and one to sell it).

If you'd like to sell your property as-is visit page 118 for more details and learn how I can make the process easy and painless for you.

If you'd like a referral to a trusted and proven contractor, send me a text to (423) 460-6111 (please, text only for this service).

I Don't Have Enough Equity for Closing Costs and/or Commissions

Selling a property with low equity can be a challenge, but there are several options you can explore to make the sale happen.

Please note that the advice below assumes that you don't owe more on your mortgage than the property is worth (over leveraged). If your property IS over leveraged, a short sale might be a good option for you **(Please see page 22 if you're interested in a short sale).**

If you just don't have enough equity to pay for closing costs and commissions, the following is for you.

You really have 2 options in a low equity situation:

1. *Sell For Sale by Owner (FSBO)*. Selling on your own allows you to keep costs down. But this option only helps you if you don't have enough to pay for commissions (but have enough for closing costs). Selling for sale by owner is complicated and is reserved for those folks that have some knowledge of real estate (more than the average person). **You can find out more details on selling FSBO on Page 110.**
2. *Sell the property to an iBuyer*: One option is to sell the property to an iBuyer because, with them, there's no commissions and they usually will cover closing costs too. Keep in mind though, that if your property doesn't have a lot of equity, they most likely will want to do some kind of creative finance deal so you need to be flexible on terms. They can also close quickly, which can be beneficial if you need to sell your property quickly. **See page 118 for more information on selling to an iBuyer.**

If you'd like to sell your property as-is visit page 118 for more details and learn how I can make the process easy and painless for you.

I Have Bad Tenants

Having bad tenants can really be a challenging situation. Maybe they are loud and disturb neighbors or whether they break other terms of the lease. They can be a nightmare.

You have a few choices when you have a bad tenant:

Give them a written warning: If you haven't already tried giving them a written and trackable warning, you should do that so that if you need to go to court, you have proof that you gave them a warning.

Give them written notice you are canceling the lease and ask them to move out: You want to follow your local procedures when doing this.

Evict them: If the above doesn't work, go through the typical eviction process in your county. **If you would like a referral to a trusted eviction attorney in my network, text me at (423) 460-6111. (please, no phone calls for this service).**

Cash for Keys: Offer the tenant cash for them to move out on a specific date and leave the place in good condition.

Sell Your Property: Now, if you don't have time to fix the issues yourself or if you discovered you just don't want to be a landlord, you can always just sell.

I'm going to assume that your bad tenants would complicate a sale by either not having the place in show-ready condition or by not allowing showings at all.

Regardless of your past history with the tenants, it's essential to have an open and honest conversation with them about your plans to sell the property. Explain the situation and ask for their cooperation. Offer to provide them with adequate notice before any showings or inspections.

If the tenants are cooperative, consider offering them some incentives that help you make a smooth sale, such as a reduction in rent, moving expenses, or a cash payment for their cooperation.

Make any necessary repairs to the property before listing it for sale. This can help attract buyers and potentially increase the sale price.

Be honest about the situation with potential buyers. Let them know that there are tenants in the property and that you're working with them to make the sale as smooth as possible.

Here are your options when you want to sell situation:

List with an Agent: If you can get the property in good condition, the tenants are cooperative with showings and you have the time, and you are open to paying a 6% commission ($24,000 on the median $400,000 property price), listing with an agent is probably going to be your best bet. **See page 115 if you'd like information on selling with an agent.**

Sell the property for sale by owner (FSBO): Unless you have a decent amount of real estate experience, I don't recommend this for the average property seller. **But if you wish to explore this option, please see page 110 for more information.**

Sell to an iBuyer: Now, if you can't get the property in good condition, the tenant won't cooperate or you don't have a few months to get a buyer and close on the transaction, or if you don't want to pay a hefty commission, you're going to want to sell to an iBuyer. **See page 118 for more details on selling to an iBuyer.**

If you'd like to sell your property as-is visit page 118 for more details and learn how I can make the process easy and painless for you.

My Property Won't Rent

I'm sorry to hear that you're having trouble renting your property. It can be a real bummer.

There are usually just a few reasons that a property won't rent:
- The price
- The condition
- The location

You can't control the location so I won't delve too much into that. Although, a bad location can usually be counterbalanced by lowering the price.

Then we have the condition. You need to make sure that your property is move-in ready. Listen to the feedback you get on the showing appointments.

Here are your options in this situation:

Tinker with Price or Repair the Property: The price can usually fix a condition and location issue. **If you'd like a referral to a trusted and proven contractor, send me a text to (423) 460-6111 (please, text only for this service).**

Sell to an iBuyer: Now, if you don't have time to fix the issues yourself or if you discovered you just don't want to be a landlord, you can always sell to an iBuyer. **See page 118 for more details on selling to an iBuyer.**

If you'd like to sell your property as-is visit page 118 for more details and learn how I can make the process easy and painless for you.

I Have Tenants/Squatters that Aren't Paying

I'm sorry to hear that you have folks in your property that aren't doing the right thing.

If you have a squatter, depending on your municipality, you might be able to complete an affidavit that they don't have a lease and the police might remove them. If not, you're going to have to evict them.

Now, if you have tenants that aren't paying, you have a few options:

Evict them: Go through the typical eviction process in your county. **If you would like a referral to a trusted eviction attorney in my network, text me at (423) 460-6111. (please, no phone calls for this service).**

Cash for Keys: Offer the tenant cash for them to move out on a specific date and leave the place in good condition.

Sell to an iBuyer: Now, if you don't have time to fix the issues yourself or if you discovered you just don't want to be a landlord, you can always sell to an iBuyer. **See page 118 for more details on selling to an iBuyer.**

If you'd like to sell your property as-is visit page 118 for more details and learn how I can make the process easy and painless for you.

My Rental Has Negative Cash-Flow

Being in a negative cash-flow situation is an unfortunate position to be in. You're basically paying for your tenant to live in your property. That definitely can't continue forever.

If they have a lease, offer them Cash for Keys: Offer the tenant cash for them to move out on a specific date and leave the place in good condition. If this doesn't work, you'll have to wait until their lease is up and then just don't renew the lease. If they are breaking a clause in the lease, you can also use that to terminate their lease and, if necessary, evict them.

If they don't have a lease, give them 30 days notice: Pretty self-explanatory. If they don't move out, you'll have to offer them cash for keys or evict them.

Sell to an iBuyer: Now, if you don't have time to fix the issues yourself or if you discovered you just don't want to be a landlord, you can always sell to an iBuyer. **See page 118 for more details on selling to an iBuyer.**

If you'd like to sell your property as-is visit page 118 for more details and learn how I can make the process easy and painless for you.

I'm Not Happy with My Real Estate Agent

I'm sorry to hear that you're having trouble with your real estate agent.

Believe it or not, many people have issues with agents. Agents make a lot of promises initially and usually try to get you to sign a 6 month contract that doesn't have any performance guarantees (basically, they don't have to fulfill any of the promises they made initially because they aren't mentioned in the contract).

Most agents will talk about their 117 point marketing plan but the reality is... most agents just put the property in the MLS and hope for the best. 95%+ of the time, it is another agent that actually sells the property and they earned a big commission for entering the listing in the MLS and pushing some paperwork.

If you've tried talking to your agent and telling them what you're unhappy about and it has fallen on deaf ears, you can ask them to voluntarily cancel the agreement. They don't have to do this but a majority of agents realize that it would be difficult to work with a seller that doesn't want to work with them.

If that doesn't work, you can always contact their broker and ask them to let you out of the contract.

If that fails, every state has a real estate commission that regulates agents. You can always file a complaint with them. Sometimes even threatening the agent or broker with this (after exhausting all other options) will get the job done.

Selling a property can be a stressful experience, but it's important to have an agent who is working in your best interest. Don't be afraid to speak up if you feel your agent isn't meeting your expectations.

If you'd like to sell your property without jumping through the hoops of listing with an agent or trying to sell on your own, visit page 118 for more details and learn how I can make the process easy and painless for you.

I Don't Live Near the Property

Selling a property when you don't live near it can be challenging, but it is definitely possible with the help of technology and some careful planning.

If you're not near the property, selling for sale by owner (FSBO) is hard because you're not on the ground to get the property ready for sale or to show it to potential buyers so I'll eliminate that from the list of options.

Selling a property remotely can be a bit more challenging than selling a property when you're physically present, but with the right tools and resources, it can be done successfully.

Here are some steps to help you sell your property remotely:

1. *Hire a real estate agent:* If your property is modern and in move-in condition and you have the time (typically 3 months to close) and don't mind giving them a 6% commission (average $24,000 commission on the average $400,000 house), then an agent is probably the best way to go. **Go to page 115 to find out more. (but read the option below first)**
2. *Sell to an iBuyer.* An iBuyer is usually best if you want to sell as-is and you want a quicker sale with a predictable closing date so it's easier to make future plans. Also, there are no commissions. They make everything easier (especially for remote sellers). **If this is of interest to you, go to page 118 to find out more.**

If you'd like to sell your property as-is visit page 118 for more details and learn how I can make the process easy and painless for you.

I Have Liens/Judgments on My Property

There are many different types of liens that can be placed on a property like these:

- Mechanics Liens
- Judgment Lien
- Bail Bond Lien
- Municipal Lien
- Tax Lien
- Etc.

Regardless of what kind of lien or judgment it is, more things about them are the same than different so I'll focus on the similarities, rather than the differences.

A lien on real estate is a legal claim or right that a creditor or other party has on a piece of property in order to secure payment of a debt or obligation. The lien gives the creditor the right to take possession of the property or force its sale if the debt is not repaid as agreed.

A lien can be placed on a property for a variety of reasons, such as unpaid taxes, unpaid contractor bills, unpaid mortgages, homeowners associations (HOA) fines or other unpaid debts.. Liens can also be placed on a property as part of a court judgment or a divorce settlement. There's also bail bond liens as well. The list is long.

When a lien is placed on a property, it becomes a matter of public record, and anyone who is interested in purchasing the property or lending money against it will be aware of the lien. The lien remains in effect until the underlying debt is satisfied, at which point the lien holder will release the lien.

It's important to note that liens can be complex legal matters, and the options available to you may depend on the specific circumstances of your situation and the state that you're in.

If someone has put a lien on your property, you have several options:

Pay off the debt: If the lien is related to an unpaid debt, you can pay off the debt in full to have the lien removed. Once the debt is paid, the lien holder will release the lien. If you don't have the cash to pay it off, you could always refinance as well. **Then you can sell with an agent (see page 115) or for sale by owner (see page 110) or...**

Sell the property to an iBuyer: If you are unable to resolve the debt and the lien remains on the property, you can always sell the property to an iBuyer. A lien holder that isn't being paid can foreclose at any time so time is usually of the essence which usually eliminates the options of selling with an agent or for sale by owner (FSBO). An iBuyer can also purchase with the lien in place as well, which makes for a faster closing. **To get more information about selling to an iBuyer, go to page 118.**

If you'd like to sell your property as-is visit page 118 for more details and learn how I can make the process easy and painless for you.

If you are behind on your mortgage payments, visit page 5 for more information.

If you are behind on your property taxes, visit page 46 for more information.

Code Violations/Condemnation/Loss of Occupancy Permit

Code violations refer to the breach of rules, standards, or regulations put in place to ensure safety, health, and welfare in a particular community. These codes can be related to building construction, electrical work, plumbing, fire safety, zoning laws, and other regulations.

For instance, a code violation in building construction might involve building a structure that is not up to code, such as not meeting required safety standards or not following the approved plans. An electrical code violation might involve improper installation of wiring or electrical equipment that could cause a fire. A plumbing code violation might involve using substandard materials or installing plumbing fixtures in an incorrect manner.

Code violations can pose serious risks to individuals and the community, and they can result in fines, legal action, or other penalties. In some cases, code violations may require corrective action to be taken, such as bringing a building up to code or repairing faulty equipment.

When you have many code violations (or serious code violations) sometimes the local government will condemn the property or revoke your occupancy certificate.

The process of fixing a code violation will depend on the specific violation and the jurisdiction in which it occurred. In some cases, resolving a code violation can be a complex and time-consuming process.

In general, here are some steps you can take to solve a code violation:

Try to rectify the violation Yourself: First, get a copy of the code violations from the building department in your local Municipality. Once you have identified the violation, review the relevant code or regulation to determine what needs to be done to bring the situation into compliance. Develop a plan to address the violation. This may involve hiring a professional contractor to make necessary repairs or modifications, or it may involve submitting plans to the local authorities for approval before starting work. Depending on the type of violation and the jurisdiction in which it occurred, you may need to obtain permits before you can proceed with repairs or modifications. This typically involves submitting plans and paying fees to the local authorities. Once you have the necessary approvals and permits, make the necessary repairs or modifications to bring the situation into compliance with the code. Once the repairs or modifications have been completed, schedule a final inspection with the local authorities to ensure that the code violation has been resolved.

Sell the property to an iBuyer: Regular buyers on the retail market will rarely be open to buying properties with code violations so that usually eliminates the options of selling for sale by owner (FSBO) or with an agent. When selling a property with code violations to an iBuyer, you'll still need to disclose the violations or it can result in legal problems down the line. And keep in mind that you'll have to discount the price heavily. **To find out more about selling to an iBuyer, go to page 118.**

Just so you're aware, this is the universal iBuyer formula on a property that needs repairs. Let's say that the After Repair Value (ARV) of the property is $200,000. This is the retail value of the property IF it were fully fixed up. This isn't a number that you're entitled to or to benefit from unless YOU do the repairs… it's just a number that iBuyers use to calculate your offer. And let's say the property needs $40,000 in repairs to bring it up to that $200,000 value. To calculate your offer price, they would take $200,000 and multiply it by 65% (you would get $130,000) and then subtract the repairs ($40,000) and offer you $90,000.

It may seem like a low offer but there's a lot of risk in renovating a property. And the iBuyer has to pay 2 sets of closing costs (one to buy the property and one to sell it).

If you'd like to sell your property as-is visit page 118 for more details and learn how I can make the process easy and painless for you.

If you'd like a referral to a trusted and proven contractor, send me a text to (423) 460-6111 (please, text only for this service).

I Have a Contract/Property I Want to Wholesale

I buy from wholesalers all of the time.

If you'd like me to consider one of your deals, please follow this process:
1. Please make sure it's an actual deal. I get a lot of deals from wholesalers that wouldn't make financial sense for anyone to buy. Please have solid numbers and do your homework.
2. Email me all of the details necessary for me to be able to make a decision on the deal. This includes many photos of the property and all of the numbers of the property (asking price, estimated amount in repairs, ARV (with comps), loan balance, your wholesale fee, etc.). Please include the address too.

Please put effort into selling the deal. If I see that you're serious about getting me what I need, I'll take you more seriously and give your deals priority.

If you send me deals where the repair estimates are underinflated and the ARV is overinflated, that's the quickest way to be put into my SPAM folder.

Please email the details to deals@PropDaddy.com

I Want to Sell For Sale By Owner (FSBO)

Some folks like selling For Sale by Owner (FSBO) because it saves them money on commissions. The typical agent commission is 6% of the sales price of the property. On the average $400,000 house, that's $24,000 (an entire year's salary for some).

But, if you're going to list your property FSBO, I would highly recommend you have a good deal of knowledge more than the average person. While I'm not a big fan of agents and their high commissions, there is some skill involved when selling property.

Selling a property yourself (and doing it right) can take a few hundred hours of work as an amateur. And that doesn't even count the time you'll spend tending to your normal responsibilities as a seller such as decluttering, cleaning, repairs, lawn maintenance, and paint touch-ups.

You should have the time to sell. Because typically, FSBO sales take longer than agent sale sales. You'll have to treat this as a job if you want to come out on top. That's why it's rare for people to go this route (just 8% of property sales happen FSBO… that should tell you something).

If you list a property yourself, you'll be responsible for the entire process:

1. *Getting it Ready for Sale*: Here's a quick list of things you should do to get the property ready for sale:
    *   Deep cleaning
    *   Make any necessary repairs
    *   Declutter: put away personal items
    *   Powerwash the house and sidewalks
    *   Clean the windows
    *   Fix any landscaping issues
    *   Paint (if necessary)
    *   Eliminate any weird odors

These activities may take weeks or even months to finish, so this is only an option for those who have ample time to prepare.

2. *Taking Great Pictures*: Fifty percent of property buyers found their new homes online. That is why a polished and organized home with high-quality photos are crucial. This is one of the areas where FSBO sellers fall short and it affects the success of their sale.

3. *Choosing the Best Price*: You really need to have a handle on how much similar properties in your area have recently sold for. FSBO sellers need to find that sweet spot. By setting a price too high, you can scare off buyers. But if it is too low, buyers may think that something is wrong or that you are pushing for a bidding war. You should never trust automatic online value estimators like the ZillowZestimate (or similar). These are known for being highly inaccurate. You also can't use the listing prices of properties currently on the market. It has to be sold prices from properties close in distance to yours and similar in number of bedrooms, bathrooms, year built, acreage, and square footage. You must be objective when pricing your property and you can't be emotionally attached. This is another area where FSBO sellers fall short a lot of times.

4. *Marketing*: Marketing is one of the most important parts of selling FSBO. This involves writing a compelling property description that gets buyers calling, putting up a for sale sign in the yard with directional arrows to the property and listing the property everywhere you can. Here's a list of the top 5 fsbo websites with the most traffic:
   - www.FrSaleByOwner.com
   - www.Fizber.com
   - www.Zillow.com
   - www.Fsbo.com
   - www.Fizber.com

In addition to signs, consider taking these actions:
   - Post ads on Craigslist.
   - Post listings on Facebook for free, or spend a few dollars to boost your ad's reach.

- Share your listing on neighborhood and community pages, like those on Facebook
- Tell friends, neighbors, coworkers and community members that you're selling.
- Take out a print ad if you're in a market where many people read a specific local magazine or newspaper.

5. *Fielding Responses*: Respond to emails and phone calls immediately, because any of them could be from a potential buyer. Remember that serious buyers want to narrow down their list quickly, view those properties and complete the process as soon as possible. If you wait a few days to make contact, they may already be under contract elsewhere.

6. *Showings*: You'll need to show the property to potential buyers and be available to answer their questions but not hound them either.

7. *Qualify the Buyer*: If you are lucky enough to find a buyer on your own, you need to ensure that they are truly qualified to buy by making sure that the have a letter of pre-approval (not just a pre-qualification letter).

8. *Negotiating the Deal*: You want to make sure you're looking at the full picture of an offer. Sometimes the offer with the highest price is not the best offer if their financing looks shaky or they aren't putting up enough earnest money. Don't get emotional about negotiations.

9. *Contracts and Disclosures*: It's best to use the same contracts and disclosures that agents use in your area. If this step is not followed, you could end up with a potential lawsuit or the buyers could walk away from the deal without any repercussions. You are required to follow "mandatory disclosure" laws for your area and make known to the buyer any hazards affecting the property before the sale is official. (otherwise that is a lawsuit waiting to happen.). You usually need to make known any mold, lead, natural hazards, and boundary line disputes.

10. *Inspections and Appraisals*: It's always good to be on-hand during the inspection so you can explain anything that needs further explanation. And when it comes to appraisals, it's best to be at the appraisal and provide the appraiser with justification for your asking price to make their job easier (and to increase the chances your appraisal comes in where you need it to).

11. *Renegotiation after Inspection*: Even a brand new house will come back with issues on the inspection. You should be prepared to renegotiate the price or offer credits or offer to do repairs if issues are found.

12. *Choose a Title Company or Attorney*: You or the buyer will need to select a title company or attorney that will close the deal. **Send me a text to (423) 460-6111 and I'll recommend someone to you. (please, text only for this service).**

Selling FSBO is a serious undertaking: It demands a specific skill set, extensive research, and a great deal of time for no guarantee you'll sell your property for what you want to. So, carefully consider the pros and cons before selling for sale by owner (FSBO).

Flat Rate MLS solution: You can also do a Flat Fee MLS Listing which is a service offered by a state licensed real estate broker that works as your access point to the MLS platform and acts as your lead generator for potential buyers for a one-time flat fee (usually a few hundred dollars). With this service, you list your property with the real estate broker who provides you with only an MLS entry-only service. All other agent services are excluded. So, you are still the seller of your property and you retain all the rights to sell it as a For Sale By Owner. And you don't have to pay a seller's agent commission. You only pay a buyer's agent commission if an agent from the MLS brings a buyer. (which will run you 2.5%-3%, depending on your area). That would cut the typical commission in half (you'll still be doing most of the work though). Just finding the buyer becomes easier. Instead of the typical $24,000 commission on the median property price of $400,000, you'd be looking at a $12,000 commission instead. **If you like this route, send me a text to (423) 460-6111 and I can refer you to a flat rate solution. (please, text only for this solution).**

There's also a hybrid solution: You can sell for sale by owner (FSBO) but also offer a commission by word of mouth to any agent that brings a buyer (which is the hardest part anyways). If you find the buyer, you don't owe an agent anything. And if an agent brings the buyer, you pay them half of a normal commission (2.5%-3%, depending on your area).

Or There's the Easiest Solution of All: Selling to an iBuyer.
If you'd like to sell your property as-is visit page 118 for more details and learn how I can make the process easy and painless for you.

I Want to Sell with a Real Estate Agent

If your property is in market-ready condition, a high commission isn't a problem for you and you're not in any rush to sell, selling with an agent can make a lot of sense.

The buyers that agents typically bring are looking for move-in ready properties. That's why a listing agent will typically come into your property and tell you what you should fix so that it has the best chance of selling to their picky buyers. The MLS is not typically the place for a fixer-upper property.

So, if your property does not have a modern, up-to-date feel or if it needs repairs, selling with an agent can leave your property stagnant on the market. And properties that sit on the market for a long time are typically sold at a steep discount because they develop a stigma around them. Buyers start asking themselves why nobody else has bought the property yet and nobody wants to be a guinea pig.

I'm not going to go too much into the positives of working with an agent because I think those are obvious. Agents field communications from interested buyers, schedule showings, negotiate and take care of the paperwork.

While working with an agent can have benefits, there are some potential disadvantages to consider when selling:

1. *Additional Costs*: Hiring an agent to sell a property involves additional costs. Agents charge a commission, which is a percentage of the sale price, for their services. This commission is typically paid by you, the seller, and will reduce the proceeds from the sale, which may be problematic for homeowners facing financial difficulties or low equity situations.

2. *Lengthy Process*: Selling a property through an agent can be a time-consuming process. It involves making repairs requested by the agent, coordinating showings, back-and-forth communication, long and complex contracts, disclosures and closing paperwork. This can result in delays in the sale process, and if your selling time frame is tight, it may not be what you need.

3. *Potential for Lower Proceeds*: Agents may recommend listing the property at higher than market value to make you think that they can get you a higher price just so you hire them and sign their contract. But listing at a higher than market price will reduce the amount of interest because other properties in your area will be a better value for buyers. And with reduced interest, you'll be forced to make price reductions and then your property develops a stigma with buyers because they think something might be wrong with the property because it hasn't sold.

Your property is probably your biggest asset. And when selling an asset of such magnitude, it is necessary to take special care to be sure it's in the right hands. The process of selling a property is long, complex and sometimes confusing, so if you're going to sell with an agent, choosing the right agent is important.

The majority of agents have very little actual experience but all charge high fees, typically 6%. Here's a tip: ask how many properties they have personally sold in the last year (not their company… but them). The lion's share of agents only sell a few properties a year and that's not an agent you want to hire.

In my opinion, you should never use a friend or family member that's an agent to list your property. I know it's tempting but it's filled with landmines (and the reality is, most agents aren't that great). And you don't want a relationship ruined because of business dealings.

If you have your doubts about selling with an agent and you'd like to sell your property as-is visit page 118 for more details and learn how I can make the process easy and painless for you.

If you want to go the agent route, I can refer you to a tried and proven top 1% agent. Just send me a text to (423) 460-6111 (please, text only for this service).

I Want to Sell to an iBuyer

An iBuyer is a real estate company that relies on data and digital technology to estimate your property value and make an immediate offer. If you accept the offer, they can close on your property in as little as a few days, if needed. *Well, you're in luck because I'm an iBuyer.*

Properties that meet at least one of these criteria is best to sell to an iBuyer:

- Not market-ready (needs repairs, not modern, title problems, etc.)
- Needs to be sold fast or on a specific timeline (you're relocating on a specific date or you bought another house and need to close on your old house by then so you don't have 2 mortgage payments), foreclosure, tax delinquency, etc.
- Doesn't have enough equity for normal closing costs and/or an agent's commission
- Has title issues or weird circumstances

To streamline this entire process, an iBuyer uses big data tools, machine learning and databases, both public and private, that allow them to compare your property with similar ones to establish the purchase price in an automated way and in the shortest possible time.

Advantages of selling a property fast to an iBuyer:

They are fast: One of the main advantages of selling to an iBuyer is the speed of the sale. The purchase offer is made instantaneously or within a few hours and the sale can be finalized a few days after that. This can be beneficial for folks who need to sell their property quickly for any reason.

Simplified Process: Selling to an iBuyer typically involves a streamlined and simplified process. iBuyers usually purchase properties in "as-is" condition, which means you don't need to invest in costly repairs or updates before selling. Additionally, the transaction is often handled digitally, with minimal paperwork and fewer contingencies compared to a traditional sale. iBuyers can save you a lot of time and money because of their streamlined process. 1 page contracts, quick inspections and virtual notaries are the norm. iBuyers provide a selling path with less resistance than the traditional real estate listing process.

No commissions: When you sell to an iBuyer, you don't have to pay any commissions because there's no agents involved. That saves you a 6% commission ($24,000 on a $400,000 property sale).

No closing costs: If you're open to closing in a more streamlined way, you won't pay any closing costs when you sell to an iBuyer. These are just some of the closing costs you will AVOID by selling to an iBuyer:
- Transfer taxes
- Legal costs
- Mortgage pre-payment penalties
- POS Inspection Fees
- Attorney fees
- Title Search
- Title Company Closing Fee
- Deed/Document Prep Fees
- Courier/Overnight Fee
- Owner's title insurance
- Recording Fees
- Survey fee
- Agent Commissions
- HOA Charges

More money in your pocket: Because there aren't any closing costs or commissions when you sell to an iBuyer, you'll typically get more money in your pocket. (you should focus on the money you're getting in your pocket though… because sometimes an agent can get you a higher sale price than an iBuyer but once you take out closing costs and commissions out of an agent sale, there will be less money in your pocket).

Sell Your Property As-Is: Properties for sale on the normal retail market need to be in move-in condition because that's what retail buyers demand. iBuyers buy properties that are dated or need repairs with the intention of making a profit. So, if you don't have extra time or funds for the necessary renovations, you can simply sell to an iBuyer.

Certainty: Selling to an iBuyer can provide you with a sense of certainty and predictability. Once an offer is accepted, the sale is typically considered firm, and you don't need to worry about the uncertainties of a traditional sale, such as buyer financing falling through or deals falling apart due to appraisal issues.

Fast Cash: In a conventional sale, getting your money takes longer (especially if the buyer needs to apply for a mortgage). When selling to an iBuyer, you can have cash in as little as a few days (if you need it).

If you're sold on the idea of having an iBuyer buy your property, let me buy your property.

Here's the process of PropDaddy.com (my company) buying your property:

Quick Phone Call & Agreement: You'll give me a quick call directly and we'll talk about your situation, figure out what you need to happen to accomplish your goals and I'll get information about the condition of the property. Then I'll make you an offer. If you like the offer, we'll put it in writing and get it locked down right on the call (please review my simple 1-page purchase agreement on the next page with anyone you need to review it with <u>BEFORE</u> our call).

REAL ESTATE PURCHASE AGREEMENT

Dated: **February 20, 2023**. PropDaddy.com LLC and/or assigns (hereinafter "Buyer") and **SELLER NAME** (hereinafter "Seller") hereby enter into this contract for sale of property (hereinafter "Agreement") located at: **PROPERTY ADDRESS** (hereinafter "Property") with the following terms:

1. Purchase Price. The purchase price paid by Buyer will be in the amount of **$0.00**, which may be approximate based on the final figures below, payable as follows: Earnest money deposit, hereby acknowledged received of $10.00

Owner Financing from Seller	**$0.00**
Subject to Existing Loans/Liens	**$0.00**
Cash Balance Due at Closing	**$0.00**

2. Closing date. The parties agree that the closing will take place on or before **March 21, 2023**. Buyer shall receive possession at closing and the Property shall be free of all tenants and personal property. Property shall be left in broom-swept condition and any personal property left on the grounds may be disposed of by Buyer and the cost to rectify shall be withheld and deducted from Seller proceeds. If Buyer is unable to close on or before closing date but intends to complete the transaction and is acting in good faith and with reasonable diligence to proceed to closing, then the Buyer shall be entitled to an automatic extension and this clause shall serve as that extension.

3. Financing. If there is an amount listed in "Subject to Existing Loans/Liens" above, Buyer will become responsible for paying the monthly payment(s) on the mortgage(s), as well as property taxes, assessments, insurance, and any other expenses related to the property. If the actual loan/lien balance is less than as stated herein, the purchase price shall be reduced to reflect the difference; if the actual loan/lien balance is more than as stated herein, then Buyer's required cash payment shall be reduced accordingly. If no cash is due, Seller agrees to pay any shortage at closing. Seller agrees to transfer tax and insurance escrows held by lender. Loans/liens being taken subject to shall not be adjustable or have balloon payments and shall have interest rates less than 6%. If there is an amount in "Owner Financing from Seller" above, Buyer shall deliver a promissory note in the amount listed which shall be paid as follows: paid off when Buyer finds their end-buyer and they acquire new financing and cash out of the deal.

4. Fixtures. This sale shall include any and all fixtures to the Property including but not limited to: heating and air conditioning equipment, built-in appliances, window shades, blinds, curtains and curtain rods, attached carpeting, attached mirrors and lights, shutters, screens and storm doors/windows, garage door openers, TV reception systems, outbuildings and all exterior plants and trees. Unless specifically excluded, all other items will be included, whether or not affixed to the property or structures. Seller warrants that property, improvements, building or structures, the appliances, roof, plumbing, heating and/or ventilation systems are in good and working order.

5. Contingencies. This agreement is contingent upon Buyer's inspections, approval and acceptance of all paperwork, termite report, leases, appraisals, tenant histories, completed title work, and final inspection and approval of the condition of the Property before closing.

6. Closing. Buyer's closing packet shall be used. Buyer shall pay all normal closing costs associated with Buyer's normal closing procedure. If a more complex closing procedure is agreed upon, Seller shall bear the cost. The mortgage, mortgage insurance, property taxes, hazard insurance, HOA dues, and rents shall be prorated to the date of sale. If the Seller is due proceeds, these will be deducted from those proceeds. Seller will provide marketable title via a general warranty deed to trustee with release of title to Buyer free and clear of all liens except loans/liens noted above that are being taken subject to. Seller shall transfer Property into a land trust before conveyance and the Seller shall assign their beneficial interest.

7. Marketing & Access. Seller agrees to terminate any marketing for the property for the term of this contract. Any ongoing listings must be updated such that the Property is not listed as for sale and does not show any sale price. Buyer shall be provided a key and access to the Property to show partners, buyers, tenants, lenders, inspectors and/or contractors prior to closing. Buyer may place a sign on the property for prospective tenants or buyers.

8. Legal. Seller understands that once this agreement is executed, the Buyer will begin putting time and money into this deal and may record a memorandum to protect their interest and may seek specific performance in the event of default by Seller. Both parties have had an opportunity to seek legal counsel to advise them in this transaction. Both parties warrant that they are not represented in this transaction by a licensed real estate broker or agent and no funds from this sale will be paid to one. Both parties agree that time is of the essence. Seller agrees to honor the requests of the Buyer as it relates to closing within 24 hours of the request being made. There are no representations, warranties, or agreements of the parties that have not been incorporated into this agreement and shall survive the closing. Any changes to this agreement must be in writing and signed by both parties. Seller is responsible for rectifying any government required point of sale violations before closing, if required. If the Buyer shall default in the performance of his obligation under this Agreement, the amount of the deposit shall become the property of the Seller as his sole remedy without further recourse. This Agreement and all provisions hereof shall be binding upon and inure to the benefit of the parties hereto and their respective heirs, executors, administrators, legal representatives, successors, and permitted assigns. This offer expires, if not accepted by 11:59 p.m. on **February 21, 2023** . Signed on the date first written above.

SELLER NAME, Seller   **n/a**, Seller   PropDaddy.com LLC, Buyer

Inspection: We'll have a brief 20 minute inspection (just to verify everything about the property is as you say it is).

A Few Pieces of Paperwork: We'll need a few pieces of paperwork from you to start the title search and create the closing paperwork (nothing major).

Closing: Closing is very simple. It will take you about 10 minutes to sign the closing paperwork with a virtual notary and funds will be wired to you.

A few things to note: If you have a property that isn't move-in ready for the average buyer and needs repairs or has title issues, you need to be prepared for a lower purchase price. There's a lot of risk in these issues.

If you have a property that is move-in ready, we can usually put more money in your pocket than an agent can.

If you need proof that we buy properties all of the time and that you can trust us to do what we'll say we'll do, go to www.BriansDeeds.com to see dozens of deeds from properties we've bought dating back 20+ years.

If you'd like to sell your property to an iBuyer like me, pickup the phone right now (day or night) and give me a call directly at (423) 460-6111 (<u>after</u> you've reviewed the contract above) and let's get that property off of your hands (and I promise to make everything easy and painless for you). If I don't answer, please make sure you leave a message (because sometimes out of the service area and won't know that you called unless you leave a message).

Referrals

I've been in the business a long time so if you need referrals when it comes to anything even remotely related to real estate, I can usually help.

I can get you trusted referrals to these services (but not limited to):
- Title company
- Attorneys
- Contractors
- Moving/Freight Companies
- Real Estate Agents
- Mortgage Brokers/Lenders
- Estate Sale Companies
- And more…

Don't just call people you find online and hope for the best. Get access to my trusted rolodex by texting me what you need to: (423) 460-6111 (please, text only for this service).

For information about permission to reproduce sections from this book, email help@PropDaddy.com

For information about special discounts for bulk purchases, please contact help@PropDaddy.com

Library of Congress Cataloging-in-Publication Data

First published by CreateSpace May 9, 2023.

ISBN-13: 9798394122552

Printed in the United States of America

PropDaddy.com, LLC
1441 Woodmont Ln NW
Suite 990
Atlanta, GA 30318
USA

CreateSpace
100 Enterprise Way
Suite A200
Scotts Valley, CA 95066
USA

My Personal Handshake Guarantee to You
From CEO of PropDaddy.com, LLC.

I wrote this book as a way for anyone with the desire to sell their property to be able to do it quickly and easily.

I fully recognize that buying a book, sight unseen, over the web or at first glance in the bookstore, requires trust. I also recognize that sometimes we buy books and don't get to actually read them until long after the return period has lapsed.

I know this book can help you in a big way (no hype about it). I don't want anything to stop you from buying this book, so I want to take all of the risk.

If you don't like the book (or me) for any reason within 1 year of your purchase, just mail the book and your receipt to me at the address below, and I'll give you a full refund of what you paid.

Use it in good health.

Best Wishes,

Brian P. Bagnall
CEO, PropDaddy.com
1441 Woodmont Ln NW
Suite 990
Atlanta, GA 30318

Legal Stuff

Personally, I'd prefer a world where the teachers and musicians make $300 an hour and the lawyers only make $20 an hour, instead of the other way around. But 'til that day arrives, I've gotta dot all the i's and cross all the t's.

My attorney (he's a vicious pit bull of a lawyer, he charges well in excess of $500 per hour, and is a terrifying opponent in court) says I need to include this, especially the stuff in capital letters. Let it hereupon be known that we're giving everyone the straight scoop.

Disclaimer

The information contained in this material (including but not limited to any manuals, CDs, recordings, MP3s or other content in any format) is based on sources and information reasonably believed to be accurate as of the time it was recorded or created. However, this material deals with topics that are constantly changing and are subject to ongoing changes RELATED TO TECHNOLOGY AND THE MARKET PLACE AS WELL AS LEGAL AND RELATED COMPLIANCE ISSUES. Therefore, the completeness and current accuracy of the materials cannot be guaranteed. These materials do not constitute legal, compliance, financial, tax, accounting, or related advice.

The end user of this information should therefore use the contents of this program and the materials as a general guideline and not as the ultimate source of current information and when appropriate the user should consult their own legal, accounting or other advisors.

Any case studies, examples, illustrations are not intended to guarantee, or to imply that the user will achieve similar results. In fact, your results may vary significantly and factors such as your market, personal effort and many other circumstances may and will cause results to vary.

THE INFORMATION PROVIDED IN THIS PRODUCT IS SOLD AND PROVIDED ON AN "AS IS" BASIS WITHOUT ANY EXPRESS OR IMPLIED WARRANTIES, OF ANY KIND WHETHER WARRANTIES FOR A PARTICULAR PURPOSE OR OTHER WARRANTY except as may be specifically set forth in the materials. IN PARTICULAR, THE SELLER OF THE PRODUCT AND MATERIALS DOES NOT WARRANT THAT ANY OF THE INFORMATION WILL PRODUCE A PARTICULAR RESULT OR THAT IT WILL BE SUCCESSFUL IN CREATING A PARTICULAR RESULT. THOSE RESULTS ARE YOUR RESPONSIBILITY AS THE END USER OF THE PRODUCT. IN PARTICULAR, SELLER SHALL NOT BE LIABLE TO USER OR ANY OTHER PARTY FOR ANY DAMAGES, OR COSTS, OF ANY CHARACTER INCLUDING BUT NOT LIMITED TO DIRECT OR INDIRECT, CONSEQUENTIAL, SPECIAL, INCIDENTAL, OR OTHER COSTS OR DAMAGES, IN EXCESS OF THE PURCHASE PRICE OF THE PRODUCT OR SERVICES. THESE LIMITATIONS MAY BE AFFECTED BY THE LAWS OF PARTICULAR STATES AND JURISDICTIONS AND AS SUCH MAY BE APPLIED IN A DIFFERENT MANNER TO A PARTICULAR USER.

THE RIGHT TO EVALUATE AND RETURN THIS BOOK IS GUARANTEED (PLEASE REFER TO THE TERMS OF THE GUARANTEE). THEREFORE, IF THE USER DOES NOT AGREE TO ACCEPT THE PRODUCT OR SERVICES ON THESE TERMS, THE USER SHOULD NOT USE THE BOOK. INSTEAD, THE BOOK SHOULD BE RETURNED IMMEDIATELY TO THE SELLER AND THE USER'S MONEY WILL BE REFUNDED. IF THE USER DOES NOT RETURN THE MATERIALS AS PROVIDED UNDER THE GUARANTEE, THE USER WILL BE DEEMED TO HAVE ACCEPTED THE PROVISIONS OF THE DISCLAIMER.

Thanks for trudging through all that legalese. Now that we've got that out of the way, let's be on our way…

.

Made in the USA
Middletown, DE
15 June 2023